Mediation and Dispute Resolution

by the same author

Mediation Skills and Strategies
A Practical Guide
ISBN 978 1 84905 299 3
eISBN 978 0 85700 627 1

of related interest

Developing the Craft of Mediation
Reflections on Theory and Practice
Marian Roberts
ISBN 978 1 84310 323 3
eISBN 978 1 84642 598 1

Mediation in Context
Edited by Marian Liebmann
ISBN 978 1 85302 618 8
eISBN 978 0 85700 580 9

Effective Self-Care and Resilience in Clinical Practice
Dealing with Stress, Compassion Fatigue and Burnout
Edited by Sarah Parry
Foreword by Paul Gilbert, PhD, FBPsS, OBE
ISBN 978 1 78592 070 7
eISBN 978 1 78450 331 4

Mediation and Dispute Resolution

Contemporary Issues and Developments

Tony Whatling

Foreword by Professor Michael J.E. Palmer

Jessica Kingsley Publishers
London and Philadelphia

First published in Great Britain in 2021 by Jessica Kingsley Publishers
An Hachette Company

2

Copyright © Tony Whatling 2021
Foreword copyright © Michael J.E. Palmer 2021

Poem on page 11 reproduced with kind permission of David Brammer.
Chapter 3 reproduced with kind permission of the
National University of Ireland, Maynooth.
Burnham and Harris list on pages 67–68 reproduced with kind
permission of the National University of Ireland, Maynooth.
College of Mediators list on pages 97–98 reproduced
with kind permission of College of Mediators.
Chapter 8 reproduced with kind permission of the
National University of Ireland, Maynooth.

Front cover image source: Shutterstock®.

All rights reserved. No part of this publication may be reproduced, stored in a retrieval system, or transmitted, in any form or by any means without the prior written permission of the publisher, nor be otherwise circulated in any form of binding or cover other than that in which it is published and without a similar condition being imposed on the subsequent purchaser.

A CIP catalogue record for this title is available from the
British Library and the Library of Congress

ISBN 978 1 78775 115 6
eISBN 978 1 78775 116 3

Printed and bound in the United States by Integrated Books International

Jessica Kingsley Publishers' policy is to use papers that are natural, renewable and recyclable products and made from wood grown in sustainable forests. The logging and manufacturing processes are expected to conform to the environmental regulations of the country of origin.

Jessica Kingsley Publishers
Carmelite House
50 Victoria Embankment
London EC4Y 0DZ

www.jkp.com

Acknowledgements

For Carolyn and our two sons, Steve and Stuart, for being just who and how they are, and our amazing grandson, Anthony William, who continues to amaze all of us. Special thanks also to my good friend Adrian Perkins who, for so many years, steadfastly encouraged me to write and so generously edited my numerous articles and first book for grammar and typos. I learned so much from him. Thanks too to my many clients who taught me so much about what they were going through, what help they needed from me, what I did that helped, and what I learned from what I could do better. Thanks too for my many supervisees and trainees worldwide, who made it very clear what sort of books they wanted me to write. Finally, my special thanks to all those at Jessica Kingsley Publishers, who have devoted so much time and effort to help get this book to publication. I did not make it easy for them. To have written one book felt impossible. To have written a second would not have happened without the encouragement and support of all the above and so many other friends not listed here.

Contents

The Mediator 9

Foreword by Professor Michael J.E. Palmer 11

Introduction 13

1. Transitions: Becoming a Mediator 17

2. Supervising Mediation Practice. 37

3. Difference Matters: Developing Cultural Awareness, Sensitivity, Fluency and Competence in Multi-Cultural Mediation Practice 56

4. Gender Difference in Thinking and Communicating and Implications for Mediation Practice: Mediating Mars and Venus. 70

5. Apology and Reconciliation in Mediation 90

6. How Mediators Do What They Do: Exploring a Range of Process Options for Practitioners in Mediation Practice . . . 116

7. The Significance of Emotion and High Conflict in Dispute Resolution and the Management of Safe Practice 151

8. Mediating High Conflict Matters 170

9. Practising What We Preach Matters: To What Extent Do Mediators Apply the Expertise of Their Professional Craft to Managing Conflict in Their Daily Lives? 188

10. The Coronavirus Pandemic and Its Potential Effects on the Behaviour of People in Dispute. 203

11. Conclusion 217

Subject Index 230

Author Index. 234

The Mediator

(To Tony Whatling: A thank you from the mediation team at HYH)

Tugging at tangled histories
The mediator living dangerously,
Strategically manipulates
Words expressed,
As a potter manipulates
Clay,
Seeking for mutual light
in the mire of
the sins of the forefathers
visited on those
Betwixt and between
Pain and solace.

Like a Conductor
Of the avant garde,
The Mediator
Normalises Thoughts,
Teases out feelings,
Promotes ideas,
Weaves dreams,
Seeking for mutual chords.

As the strands unwind
Opinions laid bare
for all to see,

The Mediator invites the players
To reassemble the narratives,
A concatenation of themes,
Bringing peace to the chaos
Transforming dissonance
Into melodic resolution.

And what of the one who seeks
To facilitate future possibilities
for others?
What gain for the court jester
who sails close to the eye of the storm?
Who inhabits the space
of heartache,
Whose labours seek for empathy
and compassion?

Ask them with open questions,
Enable them to voice their motive,
Hold their heartache,
Build their model of self,
Transform their awareness.
Become part of their becoming
And in doing so transform oneself.

David Brammer

Foreword

Disputes are innate aspects of social life, found everywhere but varying in duration, intensity, processes of settlement, outcomes and effect. The latter part of the 20th century saw a growing re-embrace in many jurisdictions around the world of the value of mediation as a form of third party intervention for resolving different kinds of discord. Despite the mediator's lack of authority to impose an outcome on disputing parties, the involvement of a mediator may well assist the parties to secure a mutually agreeable outcome by facilitating the parties' communications, effectively handling negative emotions, distinguishing between parties' positions and interests, changing the parties' attention from the past to the future, bridging the differences between the parties and devising answers that address the parties' key interests.

Tony Whatling's study *Mediation and Dispute Resolution* is a most welcome contribution to our understanding of the work of mediators and mediating. It is a gift to us all from a practitioner and scholar of immense expertise and experience. *Mediation and Dispute Resolution* explores pressing dispute resolution issues that face, in particular, today's practitioners. The complexity of disputes and the roles third party intervenors and other people play during interpersonal tensions and conflict are fundamental aspects of social relationships, and this study sheds fascinating light on the practice and the intellectual dimensions of these aspects of social life.

The knowledge, skills and strategies involved in mediatory intervention are analyzed both in general terms and with the aid of insightful case studies, and Tony's analysis conveys forcefully his deep commitment to the role of mediator and to disseminating more widely his insights about mediating, and to helping as yet inexperienced mediators to develop their own language and communication style.

The broad scope of the study, delivered primarily to the reader from a practitioner's perspective, extends from training, to the development of supervision, issues of culture and gender, expediting apology and reconciliation, practices of coworking, shuttle and caucus, handling intense conflict, assessment meetings, emotion and past history, codes of practice, understanding the ways in mediators deal with the conflicts that arise in their daily lives, regulation and monitoring of performance, practitioner and client relations, and to issues created by the coronavirus public health crisis. This book concludes on a positive note, encouraging conversations between mediation practitioners across a range of contexts and experience in a spirit of developing 'new directions in research and practice for the mutual benefit of dispute resolution and its consumers'.

Professor Michael J.E. Palmer

Emeritus Professor of Law and Professorial Research Fellow, SOAS, University of London.

Senior Associate Fellow of the Institute of Advanced Legal Studies.

Serle Court, Lincoln's Inn, and McNair Chambers, Doha.

Introduction

This book explores some contemporary dispute resolution issues that are increasingly challenging for practitioners. Some topics will be familiar, others, significantly less so. Texts on familiar topics are often outdated, and often cover no great depth or breadth. As with my first book, *Mediation Skills and Strategies: A Practical Guide*, the emphasis will be on the application of theory and knowledge to practice. It is inspired particularly by professional colleagues, who frequently describe how recent practice has become significantly more challenging compared with more traditional territory, particularly with high conflict. Each chapter provides case examples, selected so as to illustrate the application of knowledge. These examples tend to come from my primary practice arena in family mediation, but hopefully will be seen as transferable to a wide range of mediation contexts. The content in this book is designed to be relevant both to novices as well as to more advanced levels of practice. Feedback from my first book indicated that the former found it a very comprehensible guide. For the latter it was regarded as a valuable reminder of knowledge, skills and strategies, some of which had been lost from their memory and repertoire.

Chapter 1 examines the transformative pathways involved in moving from pre-existing professional roles into dispute resolution training and practice. It explores the psychological and cognitive dissonance challenges involved, and includes suggestions for managing the process constructively. Chapter 2 describes the history of supervision development. Professional codes of practice and current requirements are also explored, together with practical advice on direct practitioner observation and consultation management. Topics that were touched on in *Mediation Skills and Strategies* include diversity and culture. This is substantially updated and extended in Chapter 3 to offer greater insights into cultural differences, including clients' expectations of mediation, and their implications for practice. Gender matters are also looked at in more detail, and Chapter 4 includes more on the neurological pathways of conflict and the 'nature-nurture' debate along with implications for practice.

Less familiar areas of theory and practice include facilitating apology and reconciliation. These two concepts are explored in Chapter 5, together with potential benefits and with potential options for constructive facilitation. Chapter 6 revisits some familiar strategic options used by practitioners such as co-working, shuttle and caucus. It offers more in-depth options for managing such processes practically and constructively. It also explores controversial new models such as 'conjoint mediation and therapy'.

Managing high conflict has also been expanded upon in Chapter 7 so as to include recent increases in instances of high expressed emotion in referrals. As mentioned above, in the last few years clients are coming to assessment meetings exhibiting new practice challenges. For example, significantly more aggressive attitudes and risk assessment issues; an increase in allegations of domestic and child abuse; more complex 'conflict-saturated' histories; and more adversarial social media communications as well as communication by texts and email. Chapter 8 revisits longstanding differing opinions between practitioners regarding the relevance of emotion and past history in mediation. It explores the wider range of dispute resolution contexts, where such issues have largely been ignored in literature and training, and challenges this tradition. Training and codes of practice on this topic have generally been regarded as of significance only to family mediation practice. This historical perspective is challenged and advice offered for inclusion in all dispute contexts.

Chapter 9 explores the extent to which dispute resolution practitioners 'practise what they preach' in their everyday personal and work life and offers advice on how to manage such conflicts constructively.

In Chapter 10, important issues concerning mediation as a publicly accountable professional activity are explored together with the role of regulatory organisations such as the College of Mediators. These key issues are extended to such concepts as best practice and reflective practice as frameworks by which professional practitioners can constantly monitor and further develop their performance. Professional self-doubt, whilst often regarded as a discomforting psychological experience and 'dis-ease', is nevertheless closely linked to good quality reflective practice. Linked to the above concepts is that of professional curiosity, which provides an ethical standard for mediators that clarifies what should or should not concern them when working with clients. Continuing these themes of ethical responsibility, fundamental principles, sometimes referred to as the 'irreducible principles' of mediation practice, again seek to define ethical codes that guide and determine practitioners' behaviour. Ideas on client transitions explore the potential psychological and sociological experience of clients undergoing change as a consequence of desired, negotiated and planned progress as a reorientation or self-redefinition experience that may of itself need significant support from the practitioner. The concept of practitioner/client explores interesting links to the psychosocial support needs referred to in the previous section on transitions.

Finally, Chapter 11 revisits some of the key issues covered in the text. It highlights and amplifies some theory and practice issues and includes some links with interconnected sources. It offers some new options for managing such contemporary developments. This includes the potential for mentoring clients individually at intake, and together in joint sessions, so as to enhance constructive communications, both during and outside of meetings.

The overriding goal of this book is to continue in the style of my first book, which is to 'speak' to the reader as a practitioner. As a trainer and practice consultant, I am very aware that what practitioners want most from training and mediation literature is to know what strategies to use, and especially what to say to clients, when in difficult situations. Such 'doing' and 'saying' ideas are not intended for mechanistic rote learning. Instead, they give the trainee and novice some 'starter kit' ideas and samples from which to develop their own language and communication style. The central theme therefore continues to be to offer a comprehensive, easy-to-follow practice guide that is readily comprehensible for dispute resolution practitioners.

CHAPTER 1

Transitions

Becoming a Mediator

Some implications of making the transition from previous professional roles

It seems appropriate to start this book by exploring how new mediators join the profession, and what effects that transition experience may have during this emotional and psychological journey.

Why explore this topic?

It would be both surprising and concerning if trainee and novice mediators did not experience some level of cognitive dissonance as they progressed through the transitional process from one professional role to another.

Few mediators approach training as a first career choice. Typically, many are drawn from careers such as social work, probation, counselling, therapy and law. Anecdotally, many describe levels of disillusionment and dissatisfaction with their existing careers and the associated limitations, in particular those involved in legal practice. A typical comment is that 'there have to better ways to manage disputes and negotiate settlements other than traditional legal processes'. Some even say that had there been a viable and clear career path as a mediator, they would have taken that option rather than study law.

One of the first crucial issues to be understood by the novice mediator is that there is a major transition to be made from pre-existing work roles and responsibilities to the work of the dispute resolution practitioner. The importance of this transitional journey cannot be overstated, and yet, surprisingly, it is rarely ever discussed or referred to in mediation literature. Many who had the good fortune to be trained by John Haynes, a leading American authority on alternative dispute resolution (ADR) and family mediation, will recall his wise words on this issue during his training events in the UK. John cautioned that, when the going gets tough for us as novice mediators, what we tend to do is slip into the more familiar activities of our previous professional role. For example, if we are unsure of what to do or say as a mediator, and have a background in marital therapy, we tend to start doing some couple counselling. Alternatively, if our professional background is that of a lawyer, we may start giving some legal information, or, worse still, some legal advice. A trainee mediator is embarking on a journey during which they must develop specific knowledge, understanding, values, skills and strategies so as to be able to mediate in the style of a mediator, rather than in the style of any other pre-existing practitioner role. This transition issue should be discussed regularly throughout training, and in practice supervision, during the novice stage of development. Typically that may mean one or more years of practice experience before fully developing the capacity to operate as a mediator in a way that is significantly different from other roles they have been engaged in professionally.

Much of what follows may be regarded as overly challenging of practitioners from a legal background, and reasons for this will be described in the text. It is acknowledged that trainees from other professions such as the social sciences will also have a substantial transition to make. For example, separation and divorce mediation includes the management of negotiations on finance, property, pensions, welfare benefit entitlement and housing law. In workplace disputes, knowledge regarding disciplinary and grievance procedures and employment tribunals is required. In the context of NHS health care complaints, there is medical negligence law and medical tribunals to consider. In the main such technical knowledge can be defined as knowledge 'not for use'. In other words, mediators need the psychological comfort of having such knowledge, not least for when their clients refer to it. That is different from needing to use it overtly for advice. However, this new learning is not significantly different from some lawyer mediators' need to acquire basic understanding of family and couple relationship dynamics, and/or of child development.

CASE STUDY: Transition difficulties

One particular novice practitioner, a former London police officer, played a major part in my reflective learning, understanding and writing about professional transition issues. Pete[1] was highly trained and acculturated to the adrenalin rush of the blue flashing lights and sirens of crisis intervention, often in very dangerous situations. He described being well used to getting to a crisis scene fast, making rapid risk assessments of the situation and moving people around for their own or others' safety. Growing dissatisfaction of such short-term involvement with vulnerable people; high-stress, long hours away from his family and part-time voluntary youth work led him to leave the force and train as a mediator in his early 40s.

What was unusual was the extent to which Pete consistently and openly shared in supervision his experience of the transitional psychological dissonance he was experiencing. He demonstrated very strong people-working skills and was desperately keen to adopt the non-directive principles of mediation, yet was very aware of the contrast with his former role as a directive problem-solver. Trainee mediators must learn to adopt principles of client empowerment and non-advisory and non-directive problem-solving interventions. Nevertheless, clients frequently ask for options, solutions and

---

1 All names have been changed in case studies throughout.

prescriptions from those they regard as experts. Pete continued to struggle with his inner conflict for over a year. He demonstrated substantial skills development and was well liked by clients and colleagues. Sadly, he and his colleagues were aware that he still struggled to make the necessary transition. Fortunately, Pete was then able to obtain a social work position, working with vulnerable families and young people at risk. The role embodied generally non-directive principles but also carried a more advisory and statutory responsibility to intervene actively when safety and protection was required. I remain indebted to Pete for the learning gained from his consistent willingness to share his transitional struggle and dissonance. For reasons described below, it was unusual for a trainee and novice mediator to be so willing to share such self-doubt. This situation is an important reminder of how some of the most important knowledge, understanding and skills we gain as professionals are learned, not from books but from our clients, and in this case our trainees and supervisees.

Some typical psychological transitional experiences

From extensive experience over some 30 years as a mediation practitioner, trainer and professional practice consultant (PPC), it has been notable that many trainees and novices tend not to articulate this experience of psychological dissonance. What reasons and inhibitors might lie behind that reluctance?

A state of disequilibrium, discomfort, confusion and unease is not a comfortable place to be. This is particularly the case for those already holding other professional qualifications and experience. As professionals, our clients tend to expect us to present as confident, competent, wise, knowledgeable and skilful. The awareness of experiencing the opposite of any of these states may make for uncomfortable times for trainee mediators. Paradoxically, staying with such confusion, discomforting as it may be, is an essential path to greater insight and learning. This necessary transformation may only begin at times when we are *not* feeling in control and when there is significant uncertainty about what is going to happen next. For most trainees and novices, the outcome of this complex journey is generally constructive and leads not just to greater knowledge and skill but, better still, to greater learning and real internalised understanding.

Getting to grips with new knowledge and values and developing new skills and techniques takes considerable time, financial cost and effort. In reality, many of these skills may already be familiar from existing professional roles. What differs is the capacity to apply them towards very different outcome objectives than in one's existing roles. This contextual professional shift can result in significant self-doubts about competence. It may represent something of a paradigm shift for the trainee, an experience resulting in a sense that nothing that was known before now seems applicable. At such low psychological and emotional moments, the reassurance of trainers and supervisors is a crucial element of the bridge between past and present.

Comparing other helper intervention styles with mediation

As illustrated by the above case study, a particularly common phenomenon is the difference between existing professional roles that range across a scale of problem-solving activity. One end of this scale may represent that of a 'non-directive' counsellor. Such a practitioner would steadfastly avoid giving advice or recommending options to a client, believing the latter to be the 'expert' in their own situation. On that basis the client would, with help from a skilled counsellor, be best placed to determine what changes they need to make and how best to implement such changes. At the other end of the scale are those who are expected to provide appropriate professional advice and guidance, for example lawyers, social workers and probation officers. This group may also be subdivided according to the extent to which their advice may or may not be legally enforceable or optional for a client to take, for example by removal of a client's personal freedom or parental rights. This reference to non-directive and directive intervention is important in the sense that those coming in as trainee mediators differ according to which end of the scale they have been trained to operate as professionals. Self-evidently, those from the directive end of role responsibility tend to demonstrate a greater struggle in adjusting to principles such as 'the client as expert'.

It is not surprising that when the demands of study include competence assessment, trainees would be inclined to focus on the positives of existing competence, rather than dwell on the negatives of any shortcomings. A deeply embedded historical feature of our meritocratic education system is that it has tended to reward success and punish failings. In professional competence assessments, it is noticeable that candidates tend to present only their very best work and most successful cases as evidence. Such has been the norm for generations of students and their assessors. Personally, I tended to be more impressed with those who also provided evidence of what they regarded as their failures, especially when commenting on what they had learned from such unsatisfactory outcomes. As a trainer, assessor and PPC, a question I would frequently ask of a trainee was what were the most important things they had learned from the worst cases they ever had.

Not uncommonly, a trainee may be inclined to deny any significant difference in mediation practice from existing professional activities. Such denial is a well-understood and common psychological defence mechanism, designed to reassure a trainee experiencing transitional dissonance. Once trainees engage in practice role-play, many do own up to just how very difficult mediation is to manage, and how different it was to their 'day job'. One lawyer announced that, having tried it, he was of the view that mediating between two people in the same room seemed to be impossible. He also admitted that he felt incapable of being unbiased and impartial towards the parties.

Examples of some of the more technical differences in professional orientation that can generate disequilibrium for trainees may be worth exploring at this stage.

The use of questions as an illustration of role transition development

One particularly common example of role differences referred to above relates to the skill of using different types of question strategically. Open-ended questions are the stock-in-trade of the creative problem-solving element of the mediator task. Novices from other professional backgrounds may have difficulty in adopting the style and values of open-ended questions, in practice if not in principle. From experience and involvement with the training of many mediators, this can often be explained, as discussed above, by the other professional role responsibilities these people may also carry. Trainee lawyers in particular frequently identify the very different style of questions they are being asked to use as mediators compared with the training they received as lawyers. In the latter role, the questions they use are predominantly designed to focus on the essential facts and circumstances of a case. Mediators, on the other hand, work mostly with open-ended questioning. As such, for much of the time they have no idea what the answer to a particular question will be, especially in the early stages of engaging with clients.

This last paragraph clearly illustrates elements of difference between professional practitioners. For example, lawyers describe being trained to search for and highlight key facts. This data focus forms the necessary basis for what advice the client might need to be given, and indeed is usually paying for. It might also be essential as potentially useful pieces of evidence by which council in legal proceedings may seek to destroy the credibility of the other side; this is commonly known as an 'evidence-led' style of enquiry. One barrister described how, with regard to his work in court, he never asks a question to which he does not already know the answer. Conversely, the mediator inhabits a world wherein they are required to live with an inevitable degree of uncertainty, a state of 'not knowingness'. Hopefully, when intervening with a particular strategic question, the practitioner will have some idea of what they anticipate the outcome might be. In reality, they frequently have no control over the reaction or response, which is entirely in the mind of the respondent. Only when that response is known will the practitioner be able to formulate their next move. Mediation is to a very large extent an 'on your toes' state of 'not knowingness'.

During a radio interview some years ago, a leading oncologist was asked how he knew what to say to a dying patient and their relatives. His response was that if he asked them the right questions, they would usually tell him what it was that they wanted him to say. What he meant by this was that he had no idea about how ready his patient was to hear the bad news. From experience, he had learned to ask what the patient thought and felt was happening to their body. One patient might respond by saying that they knew they had been having some problems but that they were now on the mend and would be well for many years. Another patient might say that they felt they were in big trouble and what they needed from him was total honesty about their odds and potential time frame. Depending on the answers to the oncologist's wonderful open-ended questions, he would have learned, for each unique patient, what sort of response to give. In the case of the first example, he would know that much care would be needed and that he would probably need to confer with the patient's family as to how to proceed. How reassuring it is to know that a highly trained, technically skilled scientific medical practitioner can develop such deep understanding of how to connect meaningfully with a client at an expert level.

Note taking in mediation sessions

Another example of the unease of the role transition is that a very common concern of trainees and novice mediators is that they will fail to remember important facts and information. The concern is inevitably framed as a question as to whether it is OK to take written notes. Trainee lawyer mediators in particular have a problem with this, compared with those from a social sciences, counselling or therapeutic background. Once again, this can be understood by the nature of their legal training, from which they are expected to take almost verbatim notes when interviewing clients. To require them to stop doing this is of the order of tying their hands behind their backs, and it can cause a period of significant cognitive dissonance. So why is it so important not to be taking written notes, particularly in the early stages of the session? The answer to this question lies in the client's need to know that they have the full and undivided attention of the mediator, which is often referred to by therapists as 'free attention' or 'active listening'. At that particular moment in time the client's emotional and psychological experiences are more important than facts or details. There can be little doubt that all of us will at some time or another have the experience of talking, perhaps with a friend or colleague, about something really important, only to see their eyes leave us for a significant period. Maybe they were just distracted by something or someone else in the room. It may be that our story had reminded them of similar experiences of theirs or others. Worse still, our fear would be that they were bored by listening to what we were saying. Either way, the impact more often than not is to cause us to dry up, lose our thread or not feel important enough to keep talking.

Another writer has described this as: 'The capacity to be a good and understanding listener is perhaps the most fundamental skill of all' (Nelson-Jones 1988, p.17). Wolff et al. (1983, p.195) explain: 'The word "listen" is derived from two Anglo-Saxon words: hylstan, meaning hearing and holsnian, meaning to wait in suspense.' Hargie et al. (1981) say: 'Active listening occurs when an individual displays certain behaviours which indicate that he is overtly paying attention to another person. The second sense of the term "listening" emphasises the cognitive process of assimilating information' (p.196). They go on to elaborate: 'Different types of listening have also been defined: These can be divided into four main categories. Comprehensive listening Evaluative listening Appreciative listening Empathic listening' (pp.198–199).

From these quotations, it becomes clear that in order to fulfil all these complex verbal and non-verbal levels of interpersonal communication, the experience is unlikely to be enhanced by the distraction of note taking. The listener can always check for memory by summarising and asking the speaker to confirm accuracy of understanding.

Managing emotion and high conflict

One final example in this by no means all-inclusive list of transitions is that of understanding the normality of, and getting to feel comfortable with, managing conflict and what is often raw emotion, rage, distress, despair and deep hurt. Clients are sometimes invited by practitioners to leave fault and blame out of the proceedings, not to interrupt and to treat each other with respect. Oh come on – who are we kidding? One important key idea is that we all hold personal 'life scripts' about conflict. Depending on our early life experiences, we may regard conflict as potentially exciting, creative, energising and positive. Alternatively, we may see it as scary, worrying, potentially painful and essentially negative. Most of us will be somewhere in between these two views and are likely to say that our position would depend very much on the specific circumstances involved. (For more on life scripts, see Chapter 8, 'Mediating High Conflict Matters'.) Where we stand personally is not predictive of our effectiveness as mediators, but we do need to be aware of how conflict affects us on an individual level, as well as the effect it has on the negotiation process in dispute resolution. Other writers describe it as: 'Conflict is frightening to most people. Most professionals either are scared that conflict between clients will get out of hand and so try to suppress it or believe that it is inherently wrong and so avoid it' (Haynes and Haynes 1989, p.3). A major landmark in my own development as a mediator involved adapting my personal life script so as to be able to see conflict as potentially positive and creative. Surprisingly, nothing before mediation training, including social work, had served to bring me to have this attitude towards conflict. If such careers are not substantially about managing conflict, what are they about? Training in mediation often provides an opportunity to see conflict in a more positive light.

Opinions differ between practitioners as to how far emotion should be tolerated, or indeed even encouraged, in mediation. During training courses, John Haynes tended to describe emotion as 'un-useful dialogue'. In writing, he qualified this significantly, describing client emotional behaviour in two ways: offensive and defensive. 'Offensive behaviour is non-useful and best ignored by the mediator unless it prevents progress in the mediation process. Defensive emotional statements are often useful because they alert the mediator to underlying issues or indicate emotional issues which, if dealt with, enable the mediator to continue the mediation process, negotiating for a solution that meets the parties' goals' (Haynes 1993, p.11).

Practice experience aligns with Haynes's view to suggest that unresolved emotion frequently inhibits the mediation process and progress. It commonly operates as a covert 'driver' that may inhibit, or indeed sabotage, attempts at negotiation of settlements on substantive issues. Unless a mediator senses that, not just from the verbal discourse but also from non-verbal behaviour, one client may just leave the process. Such an action may not be at a conscious level, but rather from a subconscious sense of not being heard and understood by the practitioner. Thelma Fisher also referred to this issue:

> Any conciliator learns that conflict between couples has positive and negative power. It can create energy for negotiation or

> destroy it. The conciliator will respond to the conflict instinctively; the danger signals appear as in any situation of actual or impending conflict. Conciliators must learn to interpret these signals, as conflict is their stock-in-trade. (Fisher 1992, p.121)

Robert Benjamin also makes very interesting observations on this issue:

> Conflict is first and foremost about people's passions, desires and emotions in collision. The friction of conflict generates heat, which, like any form of natural energy, can be squandered or harnessed. The sources could be scarce resources, an inability to communicate or empathize, a moral clash over good or evil, or a power struggle of some variety. Typically they are inextricably intertwined and sometimes disguised. What is required is the deft and subtle touch of a third party attuned to the rhythms of conflict, with the necessary feel and intuition to be effective. Developing the requisite skills is a twofold task. First we must recognise the importance of moving outside the strict and narrow rational paradigm our culture has defined. Second we must find models of practice that offer support and give direction. (Benjamin 2003, pp.79–80)

Conflict and emotion in mediation are both inevitable and indeed entirely natural. Managing them constructively may be a significantly different skill than that already developed by many trainee and novice mediators. Anecdotally, lawyers working as 'collaborative law' practitioners were very open about the extent to which they felt seriously unskilled at managing high emotion and conflict in joint meetings. Consequently, they dealt with this by recruiting qualified counsellors to work one to one with each party. The counselling was designed to prepare clients, emotionally and psychologically, to behave well in joint sessions. The additional cost of the involvement of a counsellor was paid by the parties concerned. Two examples of this 'best behaviour' expected of clients is drawn from recent collaborative law practitioners' websites, which include: 'Each party agrees to act respectfully and avoid disparaging or vilifying any of the participants. A team of professionals is assembled to help the parties understand and resolve their disputes in many different contexts. The disputes may be legal disputes or emotional and include: mental health counsellors/coaches for each party, neutral financial advisors, accountants, parenting specialists, child specialists, vocational experts, and appraisers, if needed' (Beaulier n.d.). With the 'comparative law' model of practice, clients meet together with their respective legal advisors. Here, overt conflict is actively discouraged, and parties may be encouraged to appoint 'mentors' to coach them as to more constructive dialogues in joint negotiations.

It is not for me to argue about the extent to which such practice models do or do not achieve better outcomes. They are highlighted simply to illustrate the marked contrast between those writers, compared with practitioners who see conflict and emotion as natural, inevitable and furthermore functional to effective dispute resolution. One writer helpfully refers to this as: 'Conflict can signal constructive ways of bringing about change and of re-ordering lives. At least the potential for positive change is greater where there is anger than where there is the helplessness and hopelessness of depression' (Roberts 2014, p.129).

Another writer comments:

> The professional script declares that no one is to blame for the break-up. Marriage break-ups just happen: in the words of an archbishop, some marriages 'die'. Most of the clients whom I have seen do not believe the professional script. It is utterly at odds with the intensity of their disappointment and apprehension. Their marriage has not died, it has been killed. Each party vies with the other to convince the mediator, at least of the unsound credentials of the other, and at most, of her or his treacherous cruelty. Family mediators are taught that they should acknowledge emotions, but they need to do more than

this, they need to validate them. Separating people have a right to feel anger, fear or distrust. Mediators who brush feelings aside and tell their clients to focus on the future not on the past hurts will get nowhere. When clients feel acknowledged, they will be able to focus rationally on the future – not before. It is the difficult skill of the mediator to allow the expression of blame, and simultaneously to acknowledge both viewpoints, with the utmost respect. (Richards 2001, p.1)

A final word here from a lawyer mediator on this controversial issue regarding emotion in mediation seems particularly apposite:

> According to Zen Buddhism, one way enlightenment can be achieved is by holding two contradictory thoughts in the mind simultaneously. This, I have found, is more easily said than done. Perhaps I am handicapped in this endeavour by virtue of professional training. As a lawyer my mental functioning has shifted decidedly to the left brain. I know one lawyer-turned-mediator (or as the joke goes, a recovering lawyer) who describes law school as a process in which the left brain circles around the right brain and eats it. If that is the case, learning to practice mediation has presented me with the task of recovering the right-brain function, the place where creativity and non-linear thinking flourish. Indeed, restoring the balance between the two hemispheres may be necessary to succeed at mediation because the work is inherently difficult, is multidimensional, and requires not only logic but also inventiveness. The very complexity of the work is one of the things that make it so appealing: No matter how much experience we have, no matter how skilled we may become, mastery always eludes us. For people who love challenges, mediation is a natural calling. (Hoffman 2003, p.167)

What this writer is highlighting relates to theories about how people develop personal thinking style preferences. Some may develop areas of the brain commonly associated with logical, factual, scientific thinking, usually referred to as 'left-brain' thinking. Others may be more inclined to what is commonly known as 'lateral' and creative thinking, known as 'right-brain' activity. What Hoffman so amusingly identifies is how these evolved preferences tend to draw people to professions that favour their thinking style. For example, logical-preference people may be drawn to accountancy or law, whilst lateral thinkers may be more drawn towards the arts and counselling. Anecdotal evidence from many years of training shows how training for these professions emphasises professional practice expectations. Each trainee's thinking style tends to create challenges to each group in order to accommodate both style preferences if they are to respond to the needs of the client. It should be emphasised that these thinking styles are no more or less than that. In other words, most people are well able to demonstrate a capacity for either style and both ends of the scale.

Clarifying previous references to practitioner styles

The transitions debate also needs to consider issues of mediator style and models of practice. Whilst space here prevents detailed descriptions of these, most mediators will be familiar with such labels as 'facilitative', 'evaluative' and 'directive' styles.

Conflicts and disputes brought to mediators by clients are rooted in, and are in no small part a product of, the clients' past, present and future and their thoughts, feelings, attitudes, beliefs and actions, not those of the mediator. Being mindful of these essential principles in practice is to believe that, by definition, clients should be regarded as the 'experts' in their circumstances and 'subjective universe'. This being so, they are also, by definition, the experts in their own conflict and dispute situation. It follows that they are best placed to resolve the problem(s), not least because they will have to take personal responsibility for implementing any changes, actions and agreements made in mediation. The fact that spouses in the trauma of separation and being at war over their children's future care may be exhibiting something akin to temporary madness should never lead us to fall into the trap of thinking they are mentally ill. Nor should it be assumed that they need a mediator to tell them what time to put their children to bed. Problems brought to the mediator are the domain of the parties in dispute, not of the mediator. The role of the mediator is to empower the parties to solve the problems and to resist the urge to relieve client distress by assuming the burden of their difficulties. My concern about the styles other than facilitative has less to do with their application by mediators than the extent to which such practitioners may not be unaware of the philosophical underpinnings and consequences of what they do.

Facilitative mediators working in family mediation would commonly expect complex children, financial and property issues to take somewhere between three and six sessions. A key principle of the facilitative style of mediation is the understanding that clients are the experts in their own circumstances. Such mediators would be working to the facilitative principles defined above, the assumption being that hitherto the parties had taken major responsibility for understanding, deciding on and managing those important elements of daily life. Consequently they are ideally placed, with some help from a demonstrably impartial mediator, to resume those roles and responsibilities. On the other hand, some mediators, working to directive mediation styles, may resolve all such family financial and property cases in one joint session, or at most two. How do they do that? They do it by having the parties submit all financial data before the first session. The data are examined by the mediator prior to the first meeting. Typically such mediators explain to the parties that, having studied the financial data, they are able to recommend the optimum settlement arrangements. The parties, knowing the legal background of the mediator, and frequently being caught up in the turmoil of separation and divorce, are often in no fit state to question the professional wisdom offered.

Often at least one of the parties, commonly the leaver, wishes to settle as quickly as possible and with the minimum costs.

The extent to which such behaviour is right or wrong depends clearly on which position we take on the values and philosophical underpinnings of practice referred to earlier. Anecdotally in discussion, lawyers who favour this style have no comprehension that this way of working might in any way be questionable. Two particular concerns are first that we do not know how many such settlements a year or so later may be seen by one or both parties as unfair, or inequitable from their own perspective. Second, and of far greater concern, is that the parties are probably never informed as to the models of mediation on offer, or what the alternative options of mediator style might be.

Situating the above transitions debate in a theory of learning stages

Much of the above debate can be usefully clarified by a description of the stages of learning we experience when dealing with the development of complex new skills.

The four stages of learning, also known as the four stages of competence, were first uncovered by Noel Burch of Gordon Training International, although Abraham Maslow is often erroneously credited. The stages are:

1. Unconscious incompetence
2. Conscious incompetence
3. Conscious competence
4. Unconscious competence.

I have never felt comfortable with the term 'incompetence', since it feels too pejorative and generalised, especially when applied to adults coming to mediation training from a variety of other professional roles, so I prefer to substitute 'unskilled'. What follows is a paraphrased potential application of the stages to a trainee and novice mediator.

Unconscious unskilled. Here a novice practitioner, having progressed through selection to trainee, and particularly when involved in role-play, quite quickly experiences a discomforting sense of being unskilled. The experience is akin to feeling that nothing they bring from previous training or practice seems to work in this new context. It is as though they 'did not know what they do not know'. If this sense of disequilibrium and 'dis-ease' is not discussed, shared with peers and facilitated by trainers, it can become psychologically alarming, and even lead to a sense that perhaps they were wrong to aspire to this new career development and should even withdraw.

Conscious unskilled. At this stage the learner is more acutely aware of a range of skills and strategies that work in other contexts but not this one. Paradoxically, the skills, particularly for those from a social sciences and therapeutic background, are equally appropriate for mediation practice. What has to be understood is that they need to be applied to a different outcome. For example, in mediation they are not applied to problem-solving for clients but to facilitating negotiations between two or more disputants towards a client-led settlement.

Conscious skilled. This 'light at the end of the tunnel' stage begins to bring some reassurance as the learner is increasingly able to identify mediation context skills to apply to theory, objectives and values. However, it still requires a significant level of mental energy to identify what is required at any given moment, what they might have been inclined to say in another professional context and how to substitute a skill or intervention that is valid in this new craft. That analytic process may still feel uncomfortable to the novice as it can feel like something of a time lag in the conversations. Reassurance may be needed from trainers and supervisors that reflective time for all in the room is often beneficial, so it is OK to 'slow things down'.

Unconscious skilled. This more comforting stage brings a level of ability so as to no longer need the 'brain-scanning'/search energy, but where the appropriate strategy just happens 'autonomously' or automatically.

Finally, it should be understood that such learning stages are never simply a one-off encounter but likely to be recursive as people encounter new learning situations.

This chapter has explained the necessity for the experience of any major and complex professional transition to be raised to consciousness and in an open and recurring discourse. Such a discourse needs to be facilitated between trainees, trainers, experienced mediators and particularly by professional practice supervisors. The case has also been made for recognition of some of the distinctive and noteworthy features of mediation practice. It is this difference that justifies the need for significant changes in thinking and in practice, as trainees move from their previous role functions and responsibilities into the challenging, often demanding, yet always exciting world of dispute resolution. Different travellers on any transitional road should be helped by trainers, mentors and PPCs to navigate such unfamiliar territory. This dialogue should be no different than any good staff management induction process, which identifies not just strengths and qualifications, but also areas of shortcomings, so as to identify what is needed to bring them up to speed.

In understanding what mediators are 'made of' we need to recognise that they must first be aware of their own personal and professional attitudes to people generally. From that fundamental personal 'life position' they need to learn and develop professional skills and competence in appropriate client practitioner interventions, such as active listening, questioning styles and summarising. They then need to have the ability to comprehend the technical elements described above regarding the specific dispute resolution context they are engaging with. Finally, they need to have the capacity to synthesise and integrate all of these elements so that the total is greater than the sum of its parts. For a far more detailed account of these issues, see Lang and Taylor (2002).

References

Beaulier, M. (n.d.) *What Is Collaborative Law?* Mediate.com. Accessed on 12/09/2020 at www.mediate.com/articles/beaulier1.cfm

Benjamin, R. (2003) 'Managing the Natural Energy of Conflict Mediators, Tricksters and the Constructive Uses of Deception.' In D. Bowling and H. Hoffman (eds), *Bringing Peace into the Room: How the Personal Qualities of the Mediator Impact on the Process of Conflict Resolution*. San Francisco: Jossey-Bass.

Davis, B. and Francis, K. (2020) 'Conscious Competence Model of Learning' in Discourses on Learning in Education. https://learningdiscourses.com

Fisher, T. (1992) 'Conflict Patterns in Conciliation.' In T. Fisher (ed.), *Family Conciliation Within the UK: Policy and Practice* (2nd edition). Bristol: Jordan & Sons Ltd.

Hargie, O. et al. (1981) *Social Skills in Interpersonal Communication* (3rd edition). London: Routledge.

Haynes, J. (1993) *The Fundamentals of Family Mediation*. London: Old Bailey Press.

Haynes, J. and Haynes, G. (1989) *Mediating Divorce: Casebook of Strategies for Successful Family Negotiations*. San Francisco: Jossey-Bass.

Hoffman, H. (2003) 'Paradoxes of Mediation.' In D. Bowling and H. Hoffman (eds), *Bringing Peace into the Room: How the Personal Qualities of the Mediator Impact on the Process of Conflict Resolution*. San Francisco: Jossey-Bass.

Lang, M. and Taylor, A. (2000) *The Making of a Mediator: Developing Artistry in Practice*. San Francisco: Jossey-Bass.

Nelson-Jones, R. (1988) *Practical Counselling and Helping Skills*. London: Cassell.

Richards, C. (2001) 'Allowing blame and revenge into mediation.' *Family Law Journal*.

Roberts, M. (2014) *Mediation in Family Disputes* (4th edition). Farnham: Ashgate Publishing.

Wolff, F. et al. (1983) 'Perceptive Listening.' In O. Hargie et al. (1994) *Social Skills in Interpersonal Communication* (3rd edition). London: Routledge.

CHAPTER 2

Supervising Mediation Practice

Following Chapter 1, it seems appropriate to explore the historical development of mediation practice supervision in the UK, now known as professional practice consultation (PPC), which has come to occupy a significant position in the monitoring of mediation standards. One particular form of PPC, the 'direct observation' of practice, will be described in some detail and this chapter will include advice on its process management. Finally, it will explore some issues related to the dynamics of the professional relationship and processes between mediators and professional practice consultants (also referred to as PPCs).

It may surprise many of the current generation of practitioners to learn that it was almost two decades after family mediation arrived in the UK that training for supervisors finally became available.

The advent of the National Family Conciliation Council (NFCC) – subsequently renamed National Family Mediation (NFM) – in 1983 was followed by the first ever family mediation training programme in the UK in 1984. The NFCC training officer had obtained a grant from the Joseph Rowntree Foundation to design a skills-based training for family conciliation. The programme was piloted in a few UK NFCC-affiliated services that had recruited and selected teams of trainee mediators. Very soon after delivery of these pilot courses, a team of trainers, including me, were appointed by NFCC to review, evaluate and adapt that programme and to begin delivering courses throughout the UK.

These historical developments included the significant change of name from conciliation to mediation. Much of the debate in the early years had tended to focus on ways that family conciliation differed, for example from law, legal advice, marital counselling and therapy. In fact, with hindsight, far more time tended to be spent on explaining what it was *not*, rather than what it *was*. Early applications range from conciliators actively encouraging conciliatory behaviour between parties, perhaps towards reconciliation, to something more akin to what has become known as 'evaluative mediation'. In this instance, a conciliator, who may have a technical or legal background relevant to the dispute, may advise on or indeed make recommendations as to settlement options. It is also possible to find textbook definitions of mediation and conciliation that effectively read as the same activity. Eventually, in 1989, the National Family Conciliation Council changed its name to National Family Mediation. One of the key reasons for the change of name was to avoid the potential confusion about a possible link between conciliation and reconciliation, and so former family conciliators henceforth became known as mediators.

Developing standards and training in supervised mediation practice

In 1995, I was appointed by NFM to design and deliver the first ever UK mediation supervision training programme. The programme was piloted, evaluated, approved and began to be delivered throughout the UK.

This slow evolution of practice supervision does not mean that mediation practice was being unsupervised before the approval of this training programme. Previously, this supervisory role was often unpaid and drew on the good will of known practice supervisors from other contexts such as social work, counselling, probation, family court welfare and child guidance.

As head of a university department of social work education I had previously collaborated with a local authority to develop and deliver a series of post-qualifying training courses, including one for social work practice supervisors.

The theoretical model underpinning the programme derived from Kadushin, who defined three key 'tracks' that constituted a supervision process: 'Administrative', 'Educational' and 'Supportive', adding, 'with the supervisor having responsibility to deliver all three components to the supervisee in the context of a supervisory relationship' (Kadushin 1985, p.2).

Later, Garfat defined a similar model: Support, Education, Training (SET), which described supervision as 'A learning process within the overall framework of enhancing the quality of services delivered' (Garfat 1992, p.1).

Prior to designing the NFM supervision programme, I had developed these ideas for application to social work staff supervision. Kadushin's original three tracks were subsequently adapted to social work and to mediation and defined as:

1. **Accountability.** The expectation that all staff will demonstrate responsibility for the highest possible standards of professional practice and quality assurance.

2. **Development.** The responsibility to ensure that the mediator obtains the essential knowledge, skills and values, and the responsibility to regularly monitor, evaluate and appraise development towards professional accreditation and further training needs.

3. **Support.** Recognises the often complex and stressful nature of mediation and the impact on the mediator as a person carrying a range of other demanding professional and personal responsibilities.

This model of accountability, development and support is referred to as the ADS model. To that basic definition, three 'basic assumptions' were also added:

1. **Common Tasks.** There are common tasks for the supervisor in any organisation, however varied the job or context.

2. **Common Needs.** The nature of the work is such that *all* staff need recognition and support. Staff in helping organisations are regularly faced with much human sadness and distress, are often uncertain about how best to help and often work with inadequate resources.

3. **No One Pattern.** There is no one pattern of supervision that is correct for every job and context. The functions of supervision can be carried out in day-to-day contact, in group meetings, in individual sessions and in a variety of other methods and circumstances.

Having had the good fortune of attending a number of workshops by the late John Haynes, I was attracted to his 'process model', which was never published, and which I came to describe as 'alternative reflective pathways'. John described the familiar five-stage process by which a mediator asks questions of the parties, so as to uncover their issues, options and potential agreements. Typically these stages are defined as:

1. 'Engaging with the parties' – making contact with each person and explaining what mediation has to offer.

2. 'Identifying the issues' – establishing with each party their specific issues, the equivalent of a business meeting agenda.

3. 'Exploring the issues' – discussing each agenda issue in more specific detail.

4. 'Option development' – encouraging parties to identify potential future-focused options for change.

5. 'Agreement' – recording with and for the clients any interim or final outcome plans or settlements.

Haynes went on explain that in a supervision session, the PPC would use very similar questions of the practitioner, to clarify the client's issues and history. Once the client's circumstances were established, it was then important for the PPC to switch the line of inquiry to focus on the supervisee and their practice. In other words, what were the key practice issues for the mediator? What skills and strategies had the mediator used that were or were not effective? What other options might they try in future with similar cases? Rather than the PPC proposing options, they would mirror reflectively how the mediator works through skilled questioning, to help clients identify future plans. Finally, the detail of how the mediator would try that in future is recorded as a PPC agreement, to be reported back on in due course in terms of outcome. There needs to be a clear understanding of this reflective learning concept. Otherwise, it can be tempting to continue discussing the clients and their issues, history and behaviours, particularly with a novice PPC. Clients, after all, are so much easier and more interesting to talk about than the potentially more contentious 'elephant in the room' issues of a mediator's performance and competence.

To explore further this ADS model in practice, a competent and very experienced mediator brought to a PPC session the fact that he was currently involved in his own divorce. He felt that it was important to let me know this and that, whilst being under considerable personal stress, he nevertheless wanted to continue with mediation practice. He was also asking for help with monitoring his practice, and in particular his ability to maintain objectivity and impartiality with clients.

Apart from demonstrating an impressively high level of professional insight, this example illustrates the overlap between each of the three key ADS role responsibilities. A sympathetic and empathetic PPC might be inclined to move solely into the 'support' mode. Nevertheless they must at the same time retain a role responsibility for the 'accountability' function. As in this example, it is unlikely that one PPC session will interconnect all three of the ADS elements. More typically, two elements will be overlapping in any one session; in the above case example, support and accountability will be linked. It may be that the focus of any of the two overlapping elements is applicable over a number of sessions. Nevertheless, it would be expected that over a period of months, all three elements of ADS will be receiving some attention.

How did mediation practice supervisors come to be redefined as PPCs?

In 1996, the creation of the UK College of Family Mediators (UKCFM) – now the College of Mediators (COM) – gave rise to a very substantial workload for the newly formed Professional Standards Committee (PSC). For example, key priorities included establishing codes of practice standards for mediators, dealing with domestic and/or child abuse, consultation of children and curriculum standards for mediation training providers and many more.

The monitoring of practice standards in supervision ultimately resulted in a code of practice in 2003. NFM was one of the lead bodies involved in creating the UKCFM, and NFM was able to share its aforementioned work on supervision standards, models and training. Early discussions on this topic in the PSC were characterised by concerns, particularly from lawyer mediator representatives, as to any formal requirement to have their practice monitored by a supervisor. One such objector referred to the fact that he had been appointed to the post as a lawyer in his firm on the basis that he would be capable of 'practising without supervision'. The concept of supervision commonly and historically tended to be perceived as a process whereby an 'overseer' scrutinised your work performance so as to tell you what you were doing wrong.

From my work as a social work manager in the early 1970s, attempts to introduce supervision often invoked very similar perceptions, reactions and resistance. During a number of PSC meetings and attempts to formulate a code of practice on supervision, such resistances constantly resurfaced. It was eventually agreed to hold a half-day workshop on the monitoring and oversight of professional standards, designed to protect consumers of mediation. My own enduring opinion was that mediation was, by definition, a 'publicly accountable activity', and therefore, practitioners must be adequately supervised. I had less concern about what label would eventually be adopted for it, provided that the definition of the role included the three key ADS elements referred to above. Surprisingly in light of the former resistance, it was the lawyer mediator representatives who were most vocal about the need to protect the public from unsatisfactory standards of practice by poorly trained or untrained mediators. After further debate, it was finally agreed that professional practice consultation would be an acceptable title. What was more important than the label was the definition; it was also agreed that the definition of PPC would embrace the three key ADS elements, which were subsequently adapted to clarify the wording:

1. **Accountability**
   - to help safeguard clients through monitoring practice
   - to induct new mediators into the mediation profession
   - to help monitor standards for the agency and the national body
   - to challenge unethical practice.

2. **Development**
   - to support and help promote competent practice
   - to train and promote development of new mediators
   - to coach and encourage new ideas and practice

- to reflect back and encourage the development of the reflective process and of the internal supervisor
- to provide fresh perspectives.

3. **Support**
   - to encourage confidence
   - to allow vulnerability to be aired
   - to allow frustration or distress to be aired
   - to permit off-loading from within the work context and outside it, where appropriate.

The journey undertaken by the pioneers and early settlers who were involved in establishing mediation practice in the UK, its standards and oversight was exciting yet at times also fraught with complex difficulties and significant disagreement. In relation to PPC in particular, it is to the credit of all those involved that today the COM still has such an endurable, transferable and adaptive model. To quote T. Bert Lance in 1977, 'if it ain't broke, don't fix it'. It must be recognised that the value of any such theoretical model will only ever be as good as the quality of those responsible for applying it: professional bodies such as the COM, whose task it is to monitor and audit its practice. Like so many complex professional safeguarding policies, updating and enhancing PPC standards by the college continues to be regarded as cyclical and 'work in progress'.

Observed practice matters

In this section, the importance of observed practice in mediation is explained, together with some common objections to the process, and the text will offer ideas on how to manage its practice. Observed practice refers to a process whereby the PPC or other designated colleague directly observes the practice of the mediator.

Observed professional practice is not new. For many professionals, who, like Burns, might wish for the power to see themselves as others see them, it has increasingly, albeit slowly, become regular practice in mediation.

There are a number of options as to how this can be done. The PPC can sit in the room as a silent observer, taking no active part in the session; they can join in the process as a co-worker; audio or videotapes can be made of the session; or it can be observed through a one-way screen. Direct experience of all of these options leaves little doubt that the former is the ideal when compared with the others. It is relatively straightforward to arrange and offers the most effective process for meeting the accountability role of PPC and the professional development needs of the mediator. The option gives the observer scope for maximum concentration on what is happening between all the participants in the room. Whilst on the face of it the co-worker option seems more natural, and is favoured by many mediators, it is a poor substitute. The co-working observer would need to be involved in all appointments for that case, thereby increasing cost and time commitment. Making detailed notes about the co-mediator's practice during the session is not feasible. Objectivity of observation is difficult to ensure, since the co-working observer would also be making interventions. Audio or videotaping is for some an attractive option, particularly since it can be reviewed repeatedly for key learning points to be analysed. However, good quality equipment is required if all participants are to be heard and/or seen clearly on the tape. A key concern about the audio/visual option is the need for explicit policy on issues such as client consent, how tapes are stored securely, who has access to them and when they are deleted. In a worst-case scenario, it is possible that tapes could be sequestered as evidence in litigation. The one-way screen may be a familiar option within some therapeutic settings, but can be an uncomfortable experience for clients and costly to install.

The following are some common examples of the objections raised by those who sought to avoid independent observation of practice: it would change the dynamics of the session; it would have implications for client confidentiality; it would increase cost; the client would resent the invasion of their privacy; the mediation room is not big enough; the PPC would have to travel to the mediator's office, which would increase costs.

Objections that focused on problems created for the client were usually accompanied by the disclaimer that it was not a problem for the mediator. Whilst there will be elements of reality in the above objections, experience suggests that observed professional practice was usually more of a problem for the practitioner than for the client. Certainly session dynamics could be affected, but why should we assume that it would be for the worst? Issues of confidentiality must be considered, but most clients understand the nature of confidentiality being held within the context of the provider organisation rather than just the mediator. All such objections need to be weighed against the very real benefits for professionals and ultimately for their clients. Mediators are generally good problem-solvers, so issues of office space etc. are usually resolvable, assuming of course that the 'spirit is willing'.

As discussed previously, mediators who resisted the notion of submitting to any form of supervision, let alone observed practice, tended to hold negative personal constructs about the concept of supervision. Such constructs tend to be based on life experiences of critical negative feedback on performance, often dating back to childhood experiences with significant adults in authority. Supervision is often associated with professional pass/fail assessments, for example in teaching or legal training professions. Such objections also tended to assume that competence once 'proven' and 'accredited' will remain a permanent state from that point. What is needed is for those who hold such constructs to experience the benefits of professional supervision, both for clients and the ongoing professional development of the practitioner. It is to the credit of the former UKCFM and the COM in particular that professional competence development has come to be understood as a lifelong activity. To reach unconscious competence is not a linear process but a recursive life cycle that is never completed.

Returning to observed practice, after the first few minutes, the mediator is usually so caught up with the clients' issues and managing the process that they usually forget they are being observed. Clients also, at the end of the session, frequently say that they had forgotten an observer was in the room. Clients are generally reassured that mediation providers are sufficiently conscientious to ensure practice is regularly audited and concerned with improving performance.

Managing observed practice

How then is it best managed? Clients are often asked by telephone before the day, but if not, they are seen individually by the mediator on arrival. It would be explained that professional mediators have an ongoing responsibility to monitor and further develop practice. The clients are asked if they have any concerns or objection to the PPC sitting in on the session, and if either of them does, it is fine to decline. Actual words used will vary according to the mediator, but the more it sounds a matter of normal routine the better. It is very rare for a client to decline the request. When it does happen, it is often associated with early limited trust in mediation and/or high conflict or emotional distress in one of the parties. Most clients appear to regard it as common across a wide range of professional contexts, particularly for example in medical practice. As with all mediation sessions, seating and room layout are important. Preferably the observer should be out of the direct line of vision of clients, who otherwise may want to make eye contact. Office space can be a problem but ideally the observer should be as far away as possible from the participants. It is important to be a truly silent observer; for example rustling of paper or coughing can be distracting for both clients and practitioner.

The following is a copy of an A4 observation record form I designed for family mediation. Readers are very welcome to copy and adapt it, especially to other dispute resolution contexts.

The reverse of the page and continuation sheets can omit the 'Core skills observed' section. The latter can either be used to score the number of specific skills or simply serve as a reminder of skills to look for. The wording of the columns symbolises the most constructive style of feedback by the observer. Given that mediation is arguably more art or craft than science, practice is rarely totally 'right' or 'wrong', only more or less effective. Most practitioners tend to respond well to concrete examples about what was effective and what could possibly be further developed or done differently, rather than what was wrong. As standards of training have risen over the years, it is rare to encounter elements of seriously poor or malpractice. Where it has happened this tended to be based on inadequate training and competence assessment, or practice of mediation in the style of another professional background, for example giving legal advice or counselling. In the words of Rabbi Lionel Blue (Radio 4, 'Thought for the day'), 'Our successes make us skilful, our mistakes make us wise.' Or, as Burns so eloquently put it, 'It would from many a blunder free us.' It should also be acknowledged that mediation is inevitably easier to do as an observer than when sitting in the mediator chair!

Record of Observed Practice

Mediator(s): .... Service: ....

Observer: .... Date: ....

Core skills observed

Engaging	Clarification
Appropriate language	Power balancing
Child focus	Managing conflict
Future focus	Reality testing
Mutualising	Solo mediating
Normalising	Co-working
Positive reframe	Active listening
Acknowledging positions	Open questioning
Summarising	

Effective interventions	What could be done differently?

When observing co-mediators, the Record of Observed Practice form can be used to record initials when referring to individual interventions. It can at times also be useful to record the time of specific interventions, particularly in context with key movements through stages of the process. The record is left with the mediator(s). Whilst the observer would not normally take any part in the session, there can be an understanding that should the mediator feel stuck and want to consult with the observer, they can propose a short break. This does not happen often, but it can be a useful opportunity to explore alternative strategies and options. The observer may be able to provide a more objective and detached perspective on how to manage the rest of the session.

A de-briefing based on the notes ideally follows immediately after the session. The most obvious benefit is the immediacy and focus of the feedback, compared to meeting some weeks later, when the mediator will attempt to recall the details. It is not unusual for mediators to express serious doubts about their practice in the session, and most tend to be more self-critical than is justified. Working through the list of specific interventions recorded as effective can be very reassuring and affirming. With hindsight, mediators can often identify what they might have done differently before consulting the right-hand column of the list. Commonly, mediators tend not to name specific interventions or techniques that were particularly effective when reflecting on their practice. In part this may be to do with working at a largely intuitively competent level, or perhaps it is associated with a cultural taboo on self-praise. They also tend not to describe what they did in the 'technical' language of mediation, for example 'mutualising', 'normalising', 'positive reframing', etc. A skilled observer can record all such competencies directly, often with the result that the mediator is reassured to hear just how skilful they had actually been. Occasionally a very special moment occurs when the observer writes a comment in the right-hand column and within a few minutes the mediator uses that intervention. The value of this independent observed record of practice as subsequent evidence for competence assessment and accreditation is an obvious major bonus.

The experience of PPC for PPCs and mediators

Mediators are frequently faced with very high levels of emotion, distress and conflict across the increasingly wide range of dispute resolution contexts. Direct observation is a very special experience for the PPC, and often invokes a deep sense of privilege at having the opportunity to witness it first-hand.

For mediators facing their first exposure to observed practice, the hardest part is often setting the date for it to happen. From then on it quickly becomes less of a 'gremlin', and certainly requires less effort than the energy required to generate objections to getting on with it. However experienced the mediator, there is always the need for ongoing development, and for many, objective direct observation becomes something that is welcomed and highly valued.

Finally, it is worth adding a few general thoughts on the PPC experience in practice, both for mediators and PPCs. A particularly helpful concept of professional practice development is explored by Donald Schön:

> We are in need of inquiry into the epistemology of practice. What is the kind of knowing in which competent practitioners engage? How is professional knowing like and unlike the kinds of knowledge presented in academic textbooks, scientific papers and learned journals? In what sense, if any, is there intellectual rigor in professional practice…? In these cases I begin with the assumption that competent practitioners usually know more than they can say. They exhibit a kind of knowing-in-practice, most of which is tacit. Nevertheless, starting with protocols of actual performance, it is possible to construct and test models of knowing. Indeed practitioners themselves often reveal a capacity for reflection on their intuitive knowing in the midst of action

> and sometimes use this capacity to cope with the unique and conflicted situations of practice. (Schön 1983, pp.viii–ix)

Applying such ideas can usefully underpin what goes on when mediators and PPCs sit together to discuss and analyse cases, and particularly when they discuss the more complex and challenging cases.

As an example, many years ago I met with divorced parents involved in a long-running dispute over contact. Their reputation for seriously high conflict preceded them via referral letters from their legal representative, including several failed attempts to resolve matters in the courts. There were potentially very serious child protection issues, linked to the fact that the mother was having an affair with a convicted child sexual abuser. She apparently saw no reason why the children should not have regular staying contact with them. The father, who had the care of the children, was allegedly not prepared to agree contact of any sort at any time, not even at a supervised contact centre. The session was volatile from the start and required very frequent attempts to establish ground rules, such as the need for turn taking, no shouting and mutual respect communication. Neither parent showed any signs of being intimidated by the other. Despite every attempt at 'temperature control' to calm the session down, after some 40 minutes both parents erupted into a high level of abusive language and threats and left the building. My initial reaction was to engage in some metaphorical professional 'licking of the wounds'. The internal ego protection dialogue included rationalisations along the lines of that they were surely the ultimate 'clients from hell', and not even my most revered mediation guru could have dealt with them any better. After a few hours and conversations with my internal supervisor, I took a sheet of paper and started listing what other strategies I might have tried. The final list totalled nine potential alternative options. It may have been that none of these would have held any greater chance of a better outcome. What mattered was that I had engaged in the style of analysis and activity described by Donald Schön as that of the reflective practitioner.

Anecdotally, some practitioners are inclined to blame either the clients or themselves when mediation does not work. Over time, hopefully it will be possible to move to a value position of never blaming either. Instead, when failure occurs, the practitioner will engage in a reflective options analysis as described above. A more constructive endpoint for us and clients is understanding that there will be times when professionals acknowledge the need to develop a wider repertoire of skills and strategies that might result in better outcomes; in short, it is still 'work in progress'. Some examples of that ongoing professional learning curve include managing very high conflict and emotion, abusive relationships, implacable hostility or clients with borderline personality disorder. There are currently a number of examples by leading dispute resolution practitioners worldwide on such difficult contemporary issues. Such developments may challenge some of our conventional practice processes, and even perhaps some key practice principles. However, there is every reason to think and hope that over time these experiences will result in our increased professional capacity to assist those who come to our doors for help. It may help here to bring this discourse back to what happens when a practitioner and their PPC sit down together to talk about clients.

A not uncommon position for a practitioner when a case is apparently 'heading at high speed for the buffers' is to blame themselves and feel helpless and lacking in skill. In PPC sessions they duly describe the disputants and the history and behaviours that are resulting in impasse or 'stuck-ness'. From experience of working as a PPC with a young homelessness service, cases may include a highly complex cocktail of ingredients such as family violence, drug and alcohol abuse, attention deficit hyperactivity disorder, borderline personality disorder, juvenile delinquency, school exclusion, autism, domestic and/or possible child abuse, divorce and mental health issues. Commonly, multi-agency support services such as social care, education welfare, counselling and the police have at some point beaten a path to the family's door, all too often with little effect.

In due course, having recounted all the history and details, the mediator asks the PPC for advice as to what they should do or have tried. From the perspective of the PPC, they too may experience an uncomfortable sense of 'not knowingness', and indeed inadequacy, as to how to help in the role of an 'experienced and wise mentor'. Working in this particular family mediation context, practitioners face levels of such challenging complexity rarely if ever encountered by other mediation services. There are times when the PPC may elect to answer questions by saying that they do not know what to say, advise or indeed would do in that situation. The reaction of the mediator is often one of surprise, perhaps followed by a sense of relief that it may not all be down to a lack of skill on their part. At that point, a PPC may add that it is possible that nothing else will help and the case may have to be closed. Mediation is not a panacea or 'silver bullet' for all social conflicts. That may be hard to face up to, when practitioners have such a deep attachment to that which they passionately believe in and have been trained to do. However, the PPC can propose that they both talk and work together to 'unpack the suitcase', re-examine the contents and see how it may be repackaged – albeit with lowered expectations.

At such times, a complex psychological reflective process may also be operating here. When the client family is caught up in an acute crisis, disequilibrium and inability to resolve the issues, this sense of hopelessness is transferred, at a subconscious level, to the practitioner. In a supervision session this process can also be transferred to the PPC, so that systematically all involved become paralysed by the hopelessness of the situation. It is worth reflecting here on one of the key principles of dispute resolution, namely that problems brought to the mediator are the domain of the parties in dispute, not of the mediator. The role of the mediator is to empower the parties to solve the problems and to resist the urge to relieve client distress by assuming the burden of their difficulties. If mediators become too immersed in the conflict world and perspectives of their clients, they may well be no better able to see the wood for the trees than their clients. Given that this process may be operating at a subconscious level, this total immersion may be far from obvious. Consequently, the PPC must also be alert to the risk of becoming drawn in to this reflective process and recognise the need for them and the practitioner to work together to find potentially alternative pathways through the woods and trees.

Throughout the above text, reference has often been made to family, separation and divorce mediation, not least since that is where the roots of PPC in the UK are located. However, it should be noted that the same practice principles apply to all mediation contexts and are hopefully transferable. The development of the COM with its inclusive expansion to embrace all dispute contexts and ever-increasing practitioner membership has played a major part in that evolution.

References

Garfat, T. (1992) SET: A Framework for Supervision in Child and Youth Care. *The Child and Youth Care Administrator 4*, 1, 2–13.

Kadushin, A. (1985) *Supervision in Social Work*. New York: Columbia University Press.

Schön, D. (1983) *The Reflective Practitioner: How Professionals Think in Action*. New York: Basic Books.

CHAPTER 3

Difference Matters

Developing Cultural Awareness, Sensitivity, Fluency and Competence in Multi-Cultural Mediation Practice

> This edited chapter was originally published as an article in *The Journal of Mediation and Applied Conflict Analysis*, the National University of Ireland, Maynooth, 2016, volume 3, issue 1, and reproduced with the consent of the editors and publication.

This chapter will raise awareness of culture and diversity issues in the context of mediation and dispute resolution practice, provide some theoretical constructs that enable us to analyse such differences and offer some practical steps towards the development of culturally sensitive mediation practice.

Given the multi-cultural and diverse population within UK society, very little attention has been given to the implications of culture and diversity for mediation practice.

Defining culture

There is no shortage of definitions of culture. The following helpfully speaks more to its 'meaning in action' and daily life:

> For our purposes, culture is the shared, often unspoken, understandings in a group. It is the underground rivers of meaning-making, the places where we make choices about what matters

> and how, that connect us to others in the groupings to which we belong. It is a series of lenses that shape what we see and don't see, how we perceive and interpret, and where we draw boundaries. Operating largely below the surface, cultures are a shifting, dynamic set of starting points that orient us in particular ways, pointing towards some things and away from others. Each of us belongs to multiple cultures, and so we are experienced in transitioning cultural boundaries within and between us from an early age. (LeBaron and Pillay 2006, p.14)

If we extend our understanding of culture with a capital 'C' to include a small 'c', so as to incorporate a range of sub-cultures including gender differences, we can recognise the need for greater awareness and cultural sensitivity.

It is beyond the scope of this chapter to explore gender issues in any detail, yet it does rank as one of the key sub-cultural issues in most aspects of the topic. However, mediation works best when all parties are in a position of relative equality of power and are able to communicate relatively autonomously. In the same way that difference of first language between clients and mediators may, unless acknowledged and catered for, result in significant inequality of opportunity, so too may different styles of thinking and communicating.

The following quotes are included because, if we substituted the word 'culture' for gender, it effectively supports much of the focus of this debate.

> If we can sort out [gender] differences of conversational style, we will be in a better position to confront real conflicts of interest – and to find a shared language in which to negotiate them (Tannen 1991, p.18).
>
> If you understand gender differences in what I call conversational style, you may not be able to prevent disagreements from arising, but you stand a better chance of preventing them from spiralling out of control. Understanding the other's ways of

talking is a giant step towards opening lines of communication. (Tannen 1991, p.298)

A failure to address culture and diversity issues is to risk seriously limiting equality of access to mediation, and possibly risk withdrawal from the process, by clients who experience ethnocentric, one-size-fits-all communication. We and they may be speaking a common verbal language, yet conversing from significantly different cultural constructs, which may make it akin to speaking in different tongues.

CASE STUDY: A multi-cultural example

Some 20 years ago I joined a colleague who had seen each of the couple separately for the initial intake meeting. Given the high level of conflict and anger expressed by the female partner, the mediator asked me to co-work with her.

The husband, a Japanese senior manager of a multi-national company in the UK, was non-verbally expressionless and implacable. In conversation it was impossible to deduce anything whatsoever as to his emotions. Verbally he was polite and deferential in manner, yet largely monosyllabic, mostly answering questions with a 'yes' or 'no'.

His wife, who was from Africa, was very extroverted, verbally and non-verbally expressive, and frequently used a raised voice and expansive hand gestures.

They had met in Africa, been married some ten years and had two children. As mediators we struggled, on the one hand, to draw out thoughts, feelings and issues from him, yet at the same time calm her down, and manage her high emotion and constant interruptions. Finally, after some 40 minutes, she let forth a very loud diatribe of expletives against him and moved as if to attack him physically. We duly separated them and, after meeting with each, terminated the session with a recommendation that they take legal advice regarding the contact, residence and property issues.

Many years passed before I came to understand the cultural

issues presented by this case. As mediators, in deciding whether to try mediation, we had tended to focus on their behaviour and conflict styles in a traditional Western individualist mediation model analysis – responding to the overt conflict rather than any cultural implications.

How could this man possibly attend mediation and expose himself to very intimate family and personal conversations, including her very personal accusations – for example, that he was having an affair and was attempting to evict her from the marital home – and yet maintain 'face'?

With the benefit of hindsight and reflective learning, much more time needed to be spent at the solo intake meeting, exploring with each of them what, if any, cultural implications might influence their ability to use mediation. It is very clear now that shuttle mediation might well have improved the chances that he could engage in exploring such a desperately personal conflict and face challenging discourse.

In Scotland, a study looked at reasons for under-utilisation of mediation services by minority ethnic communities, drawing on information from minority ethnic organisations and focus groups, and members of different minority ethnic groups and mediators. Some of the very significant findings included:

> Everyone agreed that effective communication required the mediator to be aware of the cultural and religious beliefs of individuals to whom the service was being provided. Since communication is more than language, cultural sensitivity was seen as an important issue by most organisations. It was suggested that cultural awareness training was essential to prevent stereotypical assumptions. Culture is in constant transition and can have a range of attitudes, experiences and values existing within a single community. People from the same community with different upbringing will understand culture differently. Sometimes belonging to a particular community does not imply that the person is knowledgeable about its culture or conforms to all its generally accepted norms. Thus cultural awareness training

> emphasising that every individual has his/her own identity would be essential for mediators and workers from all communities. (Pankaj 2000, p.ix)

The core message here is that, whilst it is essential to identify and understand all aspects of an individual client's cultural experience, as highlighted by Pankaj, it is equally important to have regard for the mediator's own personal cultural identity so as to avoid assumptions based on their generalised community cultural characteristics.

Some theoretical constructs

How do we speak of such controversial matters?

A very common concern and potential inhibition when attempting to discuss cultural issues is an apprehension about which words and labels are currently acceptable in terms of political correctness.

Given the complexity of the subject and the multiplicity of literature and opinions, how do we develop awareness of particular cultural patterns, without attracting accusations of cultural stereotyping or, worse still, of prejudicial attitudes?

When discussing ethnicity, culture and diversity, a potentially safer and less controversial terminology is to speak of 'generalisations'.

> With generalizations, we look at a large number of people and we draw certain conclusions from what we see. There are exceptions to every rule but generalizations that come from research and the insights of informed international cultural experts and professionals allow us to paint a fairly accurate picture of how people in a given country are likely (but never guaranteed) to operate. (Peterson 2004, p.27)

Essentially, the key difference between generalisations and stereotypes is that the former are open to change in the light of contradictory evidence and experience, whereas the latter tend to be rigidly adhered to regardless of new learning.

Three more contemporary constructs have evolved, which provide useful tools for understanding and guiding the mediator through this complex diversity landscape: 'cultural intelligence', 'cultural competence' and 'cultural fluency'.

1. Cultural intelligence

Cultural intelligence is the ability to engage in a set of behaviors that uses skills (i.e., language or interpersonal skills) and qualities (e.g., tolerance for ambiguity, flexibility) that are tuned appropriately to the culture-based values and attitudes of the people with whom one interacts. (Peterson 2004, p.89)

2. Cultural competence

Cultural competence comprises four components:

(a) Awareness of one's own cultural worldview, (b) Attitude towards cultural differences, (c) Knowledge of different cultural practices and worldviews, and (d) Cross-cultural skills. Developing cultural competence results in an ability to understand, communicate with, and effectively interact with people across cultures. Cultural competence is a developmental process that evolves over an extended period. (Martin and Vaughn 2007, p.31)

3. Cultural fluency

Cultural fluency arises from knowing something about the lenses that we look through and then learning from the surprises we encounter as we come to glimpse the world through others' lenses. In this way we begin to anticipate, internalise, express and navigate in unfamiliar systems. (LeBaron and Pillay 2006, p.187)

In other words, as mediators we need to develop an ability to *watch, listen and think* outside of our own familiar cultural boxes, and begin to challenge our cultural assumptions.

What is particularly relevant and helpful about the above

constructs are the three key elements of *attitudes*, *knowledge* and *skills*. These could be said to represent something of a 'holy trinity' integral to the essence of this chapter, and indeed to the whole business of effective and sensitive mediation practice.

So how do newcomers to this complex subject find a frame of reference, from the maze of historical, social anthropological, sociological and psychological literature, that makes sense, or speaks to them?

Some helpful constructs

Two such frames that spoke to me more readily than others were (1) 'high context' versus 'low context' cultural communication styles and (2) 'individualist versus collectivist' (sometimes referred to as 'communitarian') cultures.

Put simply, low context Western cultures tend to have less regard for formality, titles, status or deference to community elders and leaders. For example, in Western cultures, even at the highest international levels, commercial business is commonly carried out informally and on a first-name basis.

Conversely, in non-Western cultures, 'status marker' titles are often of overriding importance. The order of entry into a room, introductions, seating arrangements, respect for seniority and titles are matters of great significance.

Augsburger succinctly describes such cultural differences as:

> Individualistic (low context) cultures prefer directness, specificity, frankness in stating demands, confrontation and open self-disclosure. Conversely, collectivist (high context) cultures tend towards indirect, ambiguous, cautious, non-confrontational, and subtle ways of working through communication and relational tangles. (Augsburger 1992, p.28)

Writing under a heading of 'Variant concepts of conflict', Folger and Jones usefully describe aspects of such differences in terms of how different cultures deal with conflict:

> For example, a major distinction between East and West has emerged in the cultural conflict theory literature... In Western-style cultures, individuals tend to view conflict as healthy catharsis for anxiety as well as a positive mechanism for invigorating moribund relationships. ... It is more honest to be open about resentment and to attempt to resolve disputes. ... In Eastern-style cultures, conflict avoidance is the norm... Whenever parties approach a situation of potential conflict either the disagreement is ignored or an intermediary is called in to resolve the conflict before it intensifies. (Folger and Jones 1994, pp.141–142)

The writers go on to say:

> In view of these cultural differences, mediators need to be ready to make certain adjustments to their concepts about mediation. Depending on the cultural needs of the disputants, mediators can sensitize themselves to recognize that their preferred procedures for interventions might need some fine tuning or even major alterations. The clients' cultural and ethnic identity must be considered. (Folger and Jones 1994, p.143)

Walter Wright (2000) usefully identifies some typical generalisations for differences between individualist and collectivist cultural expectations of mediation and mediators, which include some of the following.

As referred to above, given the differences between Western individualist and non-Western communitarian cultures, there may well be different expectations of mediation and practitioners between clients from either group, depending on the extent to which they adhere to traditional values or have become increasingly Westernised. For the traditional communitarian/collectivist client, high conflict is generally avoided. For example, in the case of a close-knit faith group community, it could be seen as representing a shaming or failure on the part of the group, or its leaders, to manage dispute negotiations and may be inclined to offer opinions and advice as to disputants' settlement options. Disputants commonly have less concern about such dispute resolvers' training and qualifications and tend to favour mediation by known and respected senior members who in turn have knowledge of disputants and their families. Matters such as shame and honour combine to encourage a culture that favours family and group harmony over an individual disputant's determination to win in dispute negotiations. Individualists, however, are generally characterised by preferring open conflict styles, regarding that as a healthy and more cathartic 'cards-on-the-table' negotiation style that is more likely to bring about change and progress. Similarly, there is likely to be an expectation that mediators will be trained, qualified, experienced and impartial and not known to the disputants.

> The conflict avoidant disputant will be likely to clam up and secretly decide not to comply with the settlement. Mediators should be wary that silence is not agreement. If parties refuse to participate, the mediator should slow the process down and caucus separately with both parties to learn their positions. Another possibility that might be encountered is that, pushed to the limits of endurance with an uncomfortable mediation, the culturally different disputant might cling to an extreme position that precludes compromise because all hope of face-saving is lost. The mediator should be aware that aggression and defensiveness can be early warning indicators that this extreme face loss is underway. Once again an aware and sensitive mediator can intervene and stop this face loss before the mediation moves into deadlock. In all cases, the mediator must remain especially observant and attentive to individual needs when dealing with disputants from different subcultures. (Folger and Jones 1994, p.158)

In addressing the question of 'How do we speak of such controversial matters?' and some helpful constructs, what I attempted to do is help practitioners understand how to address and discuss what can be of concern from a position of political correctness, acceptable contemporary language and the risk of stereotyping. From there I also aimed to offer some frameworks, through which the reader could navigate the complex maze of academic theories and literature, on cultural diversity, in a language that I personally had found comprehensible over some 20 years of active engagement, training and mediation practice with different cultural groups. Despite having read widely on these topics, direct and extensive contact with non-Western cultures brought a level of understanding, comprehension and experiential integration that was so well described by Aristotle as 'greater than the sum of its parts'.

Face, honour and shame issues

Whilst it is reasonable to assume that most human beings would prefer to avoid losing face, being dishonoured, shamed or made to feel guilty, there are very significant cultural differences that will impinge on mediation practice.

Shame is an intensely painful social experience. A Portuguese proverb observes, 'Nothing is so costly as that which costs shame.' The Bantu say, 'Shame has watchmen.'

> The awareness of disapproval or rejection by the social context of significant peers can shape behaviour, control choices, silence differences, and conceal conflict. (Augsburger 1992, pp.81–82)

The latter quotation is of substantial significance to culturally sensitive and culturally accessible practice.

In a lifetime journey towards culturally sensitive mediation practice, we are unlikely to be able to avoid mistakes – what matters is what learning we take from them.

Whilst it is reasonable to assume that most human beings would prefer to avoid losing face, being dishonoured or shamed or made to feel guilty, there are very significant cultural differences that will impinge on mediation practice. One example is described above in the case of the Japanese man and African woman. Mediation frequently involves discussion of the most intimate details of relationships, particularly in family mediation. At one level when involving a level of mutuality between clients it represents a measure of trust in the integrity, impartiality and principles of confidentiality, demonstrated by the mediator(s). However, when exposed by one party in an attempt to disempower the other, it can be a cause of acute embarrassment and shame to the other. It can also be used as an attempt to leverage for more concessions in the negotiations such as parental contact with children and financial settlements, especially where, if mediation fails, the dispute may be taken to court. As well as individual client experiences of shame it has, as described above, had major impacts on cultural groups, where it may reflect on the integrity of extended families and a close-knit family community. This idea of 'washing of one's dirty linen in public' is of particular relevance to small collectivist cultural groups living in potentially hostile and much larger host communities. Non-Western faith communities in particular have major concerns at both inter- and intra-levels. Avoidance of personal, family or community shame is deeply inculcated from an early age and throughout development into adulthood. In dispute resolution, the effect of this may be avoidance of full facts that need disclosure for settlement negotiations. Parties may be dissuaded by family members of faith leaders from attempting mediation. The latter may also seek to prescribe inequitable settlements on disputants, so as to prevent public disclosure.

Implications for mediation practice

So, as most mediation practitioners inevitably want to know, what are the potential implications of such theories to our practice? How can this knowledge be applied?

For more specific advice on culturally sensitive mediation practice, Burnham and Harris offer nine useful practitioner guidelines. Whilst not directly related to mediation, they are eminently applicable and transferable:

1. Culture and ethnicity are always important but not always obvious: explore issues of culture and ethnicity even when professional and client 'look' the same.

2. People who are different (from you) are not necessarily the same (as each other): don't assume that people from the 'same' country, family, or local culture follow the same rules of behaviour, preferences and so on.

3. Ethnicity and culture are socially constructed: as well as asking 'what is?' ask 'how do you…' sadness, joy, saying hello, saying goodbye, being the eldest daughter leaving home?

4. Hypothesising: through the process of hypothesising make your ideas, assumptions, values and prejudices open to colleagues and clients so they can be examined as to their usefulness and relevance.

5. Suspend your belief: step outside of your own cultural rules that are often 'taken for granted'.

6. Suspend your disbelief: step into other people's ideas, customs and patterns.

7. Be 'clumsy' rather than 'clever': the value of 'not knowing' and the potential of curiosity.

8. Not an educational lesson for the professional: curiosity of the professional is most useful to the family when it is related to the reason the client is consulting you.

9. Be sensitive not superficial: You have a job to do.

(Burnham and Harris 1995, p.196)

Useful steps for practitioners

What follows is an attempt to take these ideas on culturally sensitive mediation practice forward and to think about what sort of questions we might ask in our first encounters with people considering mediation. Particular words, emphasis or number of questions will vary according to the individual mediator's style and language, the particular clients and their responses:

If mediation is to be helpful in your situation, it's really important that I understand how it might work best for you and your family. So can you give me some ideas, for example, about _____? Help me understand more about _____.

- Within your family and community, how have conflicts and disputes tended to be sorted out in the past? Who in particular tends to be involved in that process, from within or outside the family?

- Who tends to have the most influence or authority and respect in that process?

- Where does that help usually happen – in the family home or elsewhere?

- Is there any difference for either you or your family in how that happens now compared with past traditional ways?

- Who else in your family, community or faith group is likely to have a strong interest and opinion as to what will happen if you come for mediation and about the decisions that you make here?

- Apart from you as the birth parents, who else, if anyone, is significantly and actively involved in the regular day-to-day upbringing and care of the children.

- If nothing from the above feels like an issue for you now, at any point when we are working together, if something crops up I do hope that you will let me know straight away.

- In addition to what I have said about not taking sides and being even-handed, I will also be trying hard to be culturally sensitive, and if at any time it does not feel like I am, I do hope that you will let me know straight away.

Finally, it is interesting to reflect that attempts to define good quality *culturally sensitive mediation practice* can result in discovering that it is nothing more or less than *good quality sensitive mediation practice* generally. That is not meant in any way to diminish the importance of raising awareness of culture and difference, but to ground it in the notion that *all* mediation practice should be sensitively designed around the particular needs of each and every individual party in dispute, regardless of the dispute context.

The hallmark of sensitive mediation practice must be to remember that however familiar the story might be to the mediator, for the individuals involved it is probably a unique, idiosyncratic, often highly stressful and seemingly impossible dispute to manage or resolve. As such, our customers have a right to be provided with a bespoke service that reflects their individual conflict experience. One size does not fit all.

References

Augsburger, D.W. (1992) *Conflict Mediation Across Cultures: Pathways and Patterns.* Kentucky: Westminster John Knox Press.

Burnham, J. and Harris, Q. (1995) 'Emerging Ethnicity: A Tale of Three Cultures.' In K. Dwivedi (ed.), *Meeting the Needs of Ethnic Minority Children – Including Refugee, Black and Mixed Parentage Children: A Handbook for Professionals* (2nd edition), pp.170–199. London: Jessica Kingsley Publishers.

Folger, J.P. and Jones, T.S. (eds) (1994) *New Directions in Mediation: Communication Research and Perspectives.* London: Sage.

LeBaron, M. and Pillay, V. (2006) *Conflict Across Cultures: A Unique Experience of Bridging Differences.* Boston, MA: Intercultural Press.

Martin, M. and Vaughn, B.E. (2007) *Cultural Competence: The Nuts and Bolts of Diversity and Inclusion.* Strategic Diversity & Inclusion Management. Accessed on 12/09/2020 at dtui.com

Pankaj, V. (2000) *Family Mediation Services for Minority Ethnic Families in Scotland.* Accessed on 12/09/2020 at www2.gov.scot/resource/doc/158076/0042757.pdf

Peterson, B. (2004) *Cultural Intelligence: A Guide to Working with People from Other Cultures.* Boston, MA: Intercultural Press.

Tannen, D. (1991) *You Just Don't Understand: Women and Men in Conversation.* London: Virago Press.

Wright, W. (2000) *Cultural Issues in Mediation: A Practical Guide to Individualist and Collectivist Paradigms.* Mediate.com. Accessed on 12/09/2020 at www.mediate.com/articles/wright.cfm

CHAPTER 4

Gender Difference in Thinking and Communicating and Implications for Mediation Practice

Mediating Mars and Venus

This chapter will focus on some key issues regarding gender differences in mediation and any implications for practice. If indeed there are differences, why might they matter in mediation and what could practitioners do to manage them?

CASE STUDY: Gender difference in family mediation
As the two female co-mediators prepared to start their second meeting with a couple, the male partner produced a pen, notepad and some index cards. One mediator asked him about the purpose of these items. The man responded with something along the lines of: 'Well, last time we were here, most of the time I didn't have a clue what you three were going on about. Afterwards, I realised that because I was so confused, there were several things I had wanted to talk about that we never got to, so I want to be able to write some notes this time. The notes on these cards are reminders of what I want to bring up, so that I can make sure they don't get lost again.'

The mediators skilfully acknowledged his concerns and went on to negotiate a compromise arrangement. In return for his not taking detailed notes, they would take more care to flip-chart key issues, check with him about understanding through regular summarising and agree on the detail of the outcome summary before ending the session. It was also suggested that if he did still want to take any notes, they would be photocopied at the end, so that everyone had a copy, and also that he should feel free to check his 'cue-cards' regularly to ensure that his key issues did not get lost.

As the PPC for the service, I observed the rest of the session. There are many issues worthy of debate here. The extent of this man's struggle to stay on the same 'wavelength' as the three females in the room was very apparent. Both verbally and non-verbally, his facial expressions frequently indicated confusion and incomprehension. The scene could be similar to observing four people in conversation where one spoke a different first language to the other three and was constantly struggling to interpret meaning and nuance.

The most noticeable difference in communication style between the couple can be described as, for the female, one of 'lateral thinking' and talking in interconnected 'big pictures' or gestalts – often referred to as typically 'right-brain' activity. The male, on the other hand, demonstrated a logical and 'linear' thinking style, and for dealing with one issue at a time – often referred to as typically 'left-brain' activity. These differences will be defined later. What was apparent, and referred to by the man himself, was that he was less well educated and articulate than his partner and the mediators. Despite this, he appeared to be intelligent and what could be described as 'streetwise', so this did not adequately explain his struggle.

A controversial topic

It should be acknowledged that this topic can be very controversial, and opinions vary widely. Positions taken for or against the hypothesis include whether differences exist at all, and the extent to which they may be open to stereotype and manipulation. Such risks will be referred to later in this chapter. However, to ignore such issues does not mean they do not exist, nor make them any less controversial. If they do exist, best practice requires exploration and analysis of any potential implications for mediation and dispute resolution practice.

So how do we speak of such things? A potentially useful theory towards moderating such differences and opinions

As a backcloth to addressing such issues, it will help to recognise the value of using 'generalisations' to avoid the negative consequences of stereotyping. This has also been referred to in the chapter on cultural difference (see Chapter 3). Without generalisations, it becomes difficult to develop debate and analysis of highly contentious issues. There are key differences between a generalisation and a stereotype. The former is open to change and adaptation in light of new data and information that challenges the hypothesis. With the latter, the stereotype tends to be maintained, regardless of conflicting evidence or new reality.

Developing generalisations has been helpfully described by Brooks Peterson writing about cultural intelligence:

> With generalizations, we look at a large number of people and we draw certain conclusions from what we see. There are exceptions to every rule but generalizations that come from research and the insights of informed international cultural experts and professionals allow us to paint a fairly accurate picture of how people in a given country are likely (but never guaranteed) to operate. (Peterson 2004, p.27)

The same writer describes a stereotype as: 'Usually a negative statement about a group of people. Stereotypes emerge when we apply one perception to an entire group' (Peterson 2004, p.26). Drawing upon the above author's comments, in mediation practice practitioners must have careful regard for both the benefits and dangers of applying stereotypes to their clients. At one level it could be argued that stereotypes enable us to make certain clusters of assumptions, formulated by our brains so as to speed up responses via our mental constructs and perceptions. A prime example of this, drawn from anecdotal experience in another professional role, is that once most adults have learned how to boil a kettle, they soon come to recognise a plethora of new designs, shapes and sizes, with or without plugs attached directly, etc.; ergo, the stereotype is functional. However, adults with learning disabilities may have training that is broken down into from 10 to 20 stages. The end result is that the student will learn how to boil a kettle, but only using that particular model, shape and design. Each new model would need to be retaught and learned, so that the kettle function stereotype can be expanded. However much we may disapprove of stereotypes and recognise their risks, they are universal, inevitable and largely unavoidable. What matters is that, when communicating directly with clients, we quickly recognise how accurate or inaccurate they are, and adapt them to the new reality. If that readiness and capacity to adapt from a generalisation to the reality fails, a stereotype may become a prejudicial perception about certain groups of people, which in turn may translate into prejudicial actions that threaten our principles of impartiality, equality and equitable practice.

Why explore gender issues?

Recognising the extent of such differing opinions, it may be fair to ask such questions as: Why raise the issues at all in a text about mediation? And, Would it not be better left alone? My own position is based on many years of mediation practice, in direct observation of other practitioners at work and through debate as a PPC. Mediation works best when each party to a dispute experiences being heard and understood by the practitioner. Each party will come with a very different idiosyncratic historical account of the dispute. Typically, each will seek to convince the practitioner of the rightness, truth and facts of their version. They will also attempt to obtain a judgement from the mediator as to their version and to their opinion as to the best settlement terms. These terms then require the other party to make all the changes of doing or not doing things differently.

Given these characteristics, the early assessment of suitability for mediation will usually involve seeing each party individually. This one-to-one time has the benefit of starting a professional relationship, clarifying what mediation is and is not and its key principles, and hearing the 'story' without interruption from the other party. Ideally, at the start of the first joint session, with the agreement of the parties, the mediator will summarise their understanding of each party's issues. What is happening throughout this process involves a complex mixture in order to construct a common understanding for all participants in the room. Of itself, this will not remove the need for detailed negotiations, nor indeed attempts to win the practitioner over to one side or the other. However, it is a crucial experience, especially that of being heard and understood impartially by the mediator. Without this complex process, the parties are unlikely to be fit or ready to start negotiations. Instead, they are likely to engage in a long, time-wasting 'positional-bargaining' argument and threats instead of the more productive 'needs-led' debate. Given all of the above, there is a strong case for ensuring that any differences in language, personal constructs and beliefs are identified to enhance equality and power-balance in communication between disputants. In conclusion, whilst the above process refers to all solo and joint mediation assessment meetings generally, differences in gender thinking and communications must also be actively monitored and assessed as to their potential implications for equitability and power balance between the parties. As was illustrated in the above case example, without that understanding and sensitivity, it may well be that one or both parties leave the mediation process feeling unable to comprehend each other, as being akin to speaking in different first languages, a factor that may have been a significant part in their being in dispute originally and seeking help.

CASE STUDY: Gender difference in workplace mediation

The dispute was between a young Muslim woman and her line manager, working in a manufacturing company, and involved grievance procedures. The incident that triggered the process involved the line manager remonstrating with the woman over her poor time-keeping in front of several work colleagues. The manager allegedly prided himself on his outspoken and forthright communication style. He associated this with qualities of good management and 'getting the job done'. The woman, on the other hand, was shy, and her use of English somewhat limited. She had been very upset by the incident, especially since it happened in front of her colleagues.

She had a period of sick leave, could not face up to seeing the manager again and was advised by her union representative to initiate grievance proceedings. The case was presented by a recently trained novice male workplace mediator at a training workshop on developing cultural awareness and competence. Interestingly, as with the line manager, he also prided himself on being a straight-talker. He described how he had tried hard to gather the details of the incident and had sympathy with her position. Apparently, her whole family were involved with running the family business full time. She, as the youngest, was the primary carer for her frail, elderly grandmother. This lady was collected every day and taken to a day centre. Unfortunately, the transport was frequently delayed, which in turn resulted in the time-keeping issues for the young woman.

Having presented the case details to the group, the mediator added that he had struggled to get on the same wavelength as her. After some 30 minutes he had been unable to comprehend her issues, needs and hopes for mediation. She had been clear that she would find it seriously intimidating to be in the same room as the manager.

She doubted that she would be able to speak up for herself and wondered if it could be done by shuttle mediation, as suggested by her union rep. If not, she asked if one of her brothers could be with her in any meetings. The mediator had informed her that normally only the disputants would be involved in the meeting. He also explained that mediation only really worked in joint sessions. At that point, she became distressed and tearful, and he suggested that she go away and write down her issues and goals.

Both of her requests should have been considered carefully as potentially appropriate options. This should have included an exploration of the advantages and disadvantages of shuttle mediation. For example, statistically shuttle mediation is far less likely to result in an agreement than face-to-face mediation. This exploration should also include what steps mediators would take to ensure the power balance between the parties in the room. Frequently, when a client asks for shuttle, the discussion results in reassurance about the responsibilities of the mediator and a willingness to try a joint session. However, the discussion should not be designed to coerce the client where they remain genuinely apprehensive about a joint session. In which case, practitioners will often encourage starting with shuttle mediation, with a hope that it will encourage a move towards subsequent joint sessions. The role of the brother at the meeting should also have been explored to ensure that she would be empowered to speak for herself, being reassured by his presence, rather than leaving all negotiations to him. Finally, the responses of the other party to these options would need to be considered and negotiated with him.

The mediator's more experienced colleagues at the workshop rounded on him, for his lack of awareness, understanding and reactions. That was tough for him, but as the trainer it was a gift, as material for the topic of the workshop, and it undoubtedly contributed to some important learning for all present.

This case demonstrates several layers of complexity, starting with the choice of a male mediator, based on the referral information. It goes too to the different gender thinking and communication styles at the centre of this chapter. The manager and mediator both demonstrated stereotypical male left-brain logical thinking and communication styles. She, on the other hand, demonstrated a typically right-brain lateral preference thinking style. The case also illustrates significantly different cultural and language issues related to family structures, norms and roles. For a more detailed discussion of these issues see Chapter 3, 'Difference Matters'.

To return to the focus of this chapter, I had been interested for some time in gender communication issues in mediation and had run several workshops on the topic. My primary influences on this topic came from writers such as Deborah Tannen (1991) and the work of Deborah Borisoff and David Victor (1989). Many people will also be familiar with *Men Are from Mars, Women Are from Venus* by John Gray (1992). Seeing these issues acted out in mediation took me back to these and other writers in the field of linguistics and communication to develop greater awareness and understanding about the possible implications for practice.

Some anecdotal evidence

Try asking a mixed-gender audience for all those who, from their everyday experience, believe that women and men think and communicate differently to put their hands up. You will almost certainly find that the majority of women will have one or both hands in the air in a split second. Men, on the other hand, will commonly be slower to react, perhaps having one hand half-up, as if unsure quite how to respond. Looking perplexed, they tend to say that it all depends on the circumstances, or that we need to explore this from a more theoretical perspective.

Some helpful theoretical examples

What scientific evidence is there of possible biological and physiological differences, for example the 'nature versus nurture' debate? Are such differences genetically or socially constructed?

If we start from a position of thinking that there are such differences, we can speculate about the extent to which they are the result of nature and genetic make-up. Conversely, they may be socially derived and the result of nurture as a result of sex-role stereotyping, or indeed some complex combination of the two.

What follows is a sample of some of the evidence from the literature. In their book, Allan and Barbara Pease assert: 'In this book, you will see how science confirms that men and women are profoundly different both physically and mentally – they are *not* the same. We have investigated the research of leading palaeontologists, ethnologists, psychologists, biologists and neuroscientists. The brain differences between women and men are now clear, beyond all speculation, prejudice and reasonable doubt' (Pease and Pease 1998, p.7).

They go on to acknowledge and give examples of how, for much of the 20th century, psychology and sociology proposed that our behaviour and preferences were the result of social conditioning. They also describe chromosomal differences in the process of determining the gender during developments in the uterus (Pease and Pease 1998). Such writers tend to acknowledge that our understanding of brain functioning is still very basic; however, it is now clear that the right hemisphere of the brain is the more creative side and controls the left side of the body. The left hemisphere controls logic, reason, speech and the right side of the body. Much of the early understanding of these differences came from studies of brain-damaged patients. Men who had suffered injury to the left side of the brain frequently lost much or all of their speech and vocabulary skills. However, women who experienced similar brain damage did not suffer speech loss to the same extent, indicating that women have more than one centre for speech.

A neurologist explains that subsequent developments in the use of MRI brain-scanning equipment has led to far greater evidence in differences between men and women. For example, the location in the brain of centres controlling not only speech but emotion, and in particular how the bundle of nerves connecting the right and left hemispheres of the brain, the Corpus Callosum, is significantly thicker, with up to 30% more connections in women than men (Gorski, in Pease and Pease 1998). Gorski went on to show that men and women use different parts of the brain when working on the same task. Pease adds: 'Research also reveals that the female hormone oestrogen prompts more nerve cells to grow more connections within the brain and between the two hemispheres' (Pease and Pease 1998, p.57).

As a generalisation, such findings appear to offer a possible explanation of a greater capacity for what has become known as 'multi-tasking', commonly associated with women (however, more recent research has failed to replicate the results from the original 1982 study that purported these differences). It may also be linked to a greater capacity to assess people and situations intuitively. Men, on the other hand, incline more towards the 'one job at a time' default position. 'Statistically, it is estimated that about 85% of males have mainly "male-wired" brains and about 10–15% have brains that are "feminised" to a greater or lesser extent' (Pease and Pease 1998, p.63). The reader may care to answer the 30 multiple-choice questions of the 'Brain-Wiring Test' included in their book to see where they are on the scale, and, knowing themselves as they do, consider the extent to which the results are as they might have predicted.

Ben Greenstein gives a very similar explanation on chromosomal differences and concludes: 'Whether one likes to hear it or not, there is no doubt that the brains of most, if not all mammals, are sexually differentiated in structure. That is to say, the wiring is different in males and females' (Greenstein 1993, p.49). Given that I have previously acknowledged the controversial nature of this gender difference debate and of different writers' opinions, Greenstein usefully offers another reputable scientific biological opinion as to differences between male and female brain wiring differences, and their links to hormonal effects during foetal development. In identifying such expert opinions, it should be understood that they are not to be seen as absolutes but instead as rating scales, from stereotypical male wiring at one end and female wiring at the other. As I have clarified earlier, most people occupy positions somewhere between such poles, and indeed, some cross the centre line either way. Consequently, they should be regarded as positional-style preferences, as opposed to fixed and immovable positions. Most people are capable of thinking and behaving with different characteristics when particular circumstances require it of them.

What other scientific theories might help to explain gender differences in thinking and communicating?

Traits assigned to men or women on the basis of gender are referred to as sex-trait stereotypes. Williams and Best (1982, p.16) define *sex-trait stereotypes* as those 'psychological characteristics or behavioural traits that are believed to characterize men with much greater (or lesser) frequency than they characterise women'. As part of their extensive pan-cultural study of sex-stereotyping in 29 countries, these psychologists found that in all participating nations, the adjectives 'adventurous', 'dominant', 'forceful', 'independent', 'masculine', 'and "strong-willed", were applied to men, while the terms "emotional", "sentimental", "submissive", and "superstitious" were used consistently to describe women' (Borisoff and Victor 1989, p.86). The authors also make the point that if we understand the nature and potential effects of such stereotypes, we can consider (1) the extent to which they apply to us as individuals and (2) the effect they may have on interpersonal communication and sex-role expectations (SREs). Whilst their focus of application is on conflict in the workplace, we can equally apply these ideas to communication and SREs in our work as mediators in other dispute resolution contexts.

How do we acquire these gender differences in ways of thinking and behaving? How do cultures convey these differences? Is it 'nature' or 'nurture'? What is it that happens to children to perpetuate such differences, even when parents work hard to try to prevent that happening? Such parents should not underestimate the many influences children are exposed to outside of the nuclear family home and immediate proximity of their parents, for example extended family members, friends and other significant adults such as teachers.

A common problem with some earlier writers on this subject was the tendency to pathologise such female/male communication differences as right or wrong, good or bad. Writers referred to here, however, tend to take the view that it is not about making such judgements but instead about facing the reality that difference just *is*. Moving on from that assumption we can look more constructively at ways to live and work with the differences, as proposed by one writer:

> Recognising gender differences frees individuals from the burden of individual pathology. Many women and men feel dissatisfied with their close relationships and become even more frustrated when they try to talk things out. Taking a *sociolinguistic* approach to relationships makes it possible to explain these dissatisfactions without accusing anyone of being crazy or wrong and without blaming-or-discarding the relationship. If we can recognise and understand the differences between us, we can take them into account, adjust to and learn from each other's styles. (Tannen 1991, p.17)

> If we can sort out differences of conversational style, we will be in a better position to confront real conflicts of interest and to find a shared language in which to negotiate them. (Tannen 1991, p.18)

As practitioners attempting to raise awareness of different communication styles, we must also have regard for inevitable 'unconscious biases'.

> Unconscious bias (or implicit bias) is often defined as prejudice or unsupported judgments in favor of or against one thing, person, or group as compared to another, in a way that is usually

considered unfair. As a result of unconscious biases, certain people benefit and other people are penalized. Unconscious biases are social stereotypes about certain groups of people that individuals form outside their conscious awareness. Everyone holds unconscious beliefs about various social and identity groups, and these biases stem from one's tendency to organize social worlds by categorizing. (Vanderbilt n.d.)

Unconscious bias is far more prevalent than conscious prejudice and is often incompatible with one's conscious values. Certain scenarios can activate unconscious attitudes and beliefs. For example, biases may be more prevalent when multi-tasking or working under time pressure. Luskin also elaborates:

The presence of unconscious bias has now been validated through magnetic resonance imaging (MRI), making unconscious bias an increasingly 'hot topic' that is heightening awareness and contributing to progress in understanding, diminishing, and even eliminating bias. ... Psychologists have identified implicit, unconscious biases. Some can be the result of repeated and pervasive messages that establish and perpetuate stereotypes. We are all biased, whether we are conscious of our stereotypes or not, so we should acknowledge this and strive to understand biases in order to deal with them appropriately. (Luskin 2016)

Once again, these writers usefully underscore and validate the core message of this chapter. As communication facilitators, mediators must have regard for managing difference. However well mediator core training may have addressed diversity, prejudice and stereotypes, I have yet to find a curriculum that includes the highly applicable theory of unconscious bias.

So, what are the potential implications for mediation practice?

As referred to in other parts of this book, the late highly influential writer and trainer John Haynes would, in practice seminars and workshops, frequently ask 'So what?' He would not say in a traditional Western sub-cultural negative sense of 'tough luck; deal with it', but in the sense of 'So, what are the implications of what we have just seen or heard, for what we say or do next?' That brilliantly simple question has become central to my reflective practice and work as a mediator, trainer and PPC. Whatever our personal opinions and values about thinking and communication differences, there is now a strong and clear case for considering their implications for mediation practice. For example, just as we would respond sensitively to the needs of a client who did not have English as a first language, or a hearing or visual impairment, so too should we have regard for significant differences in conceptual thinking and communication preferences.

It is important to add at this stage that very few people occupy the female-male gender stereotypical positions described by the writers quoted above. Most of us are somewhere between the male–female extremities of the scale and the centre point. Indeed some may cross over the central point in our brain wiring configurations. In practice, we will see clients whose communication style preferences can be seen to be close to convergence, nearer the centre of the scale and fairly well balanced in terms of left brain/right brain preferences. At other times, the more stereotypical characteristics observed in the case study above can be observed. Less often, we may meet disputants where each appears to have crossed over the centre point. For example, in a case where the father was the primary carer and full-time homemaker, and the mother was the primary breadwinner, both parents demonstrated thinking and communication styles commonly associated with other gender-stereotypical brain configurations. The father was thinking and speaking in typically feminised brain-wiring styles and right-brained 'big pictures'. The mother, on the other hand, talked in a very logical, pragmatic 'one thing at a time' left-brain style. It was interesting to note that in terms of professional career choice, the father had a background in the arts and the mother was an accountant. In terms of equality, power balance and inclusive mediation practice, what matters is that mediators have sufficient awareness, sensitivity and competence to be able to respond appropriately, just as they would to more obvious language, cultural or special needs communication differences.

Some practice guidance on such issues

The list that follows offers some mediation practitioner guidelines:

- Don't assume that because people look like you they are like you. Treat every client as unique and avoid stereotypical and unconscious bias assumptions.

- Be prepared to listen, think and communicate outside of your own communication style box.

- Client problems with communication are primarily an issue of concern for the professional, not that of the clients. It is our responsibility to understand them and respond sensitively as facilitators of effective communication.

- One size does not fit all – most, if not all, clients need bespoke designed packages and styles of communication tailored to their needs.

- Regularly audit the process and, when in doubt, be professionally curious. Suggest pausing for a while on the issue being discussed and look at how the communication and negotiations are going. For example, if the verbal and non-verbal communication indicates a potential problem, ask each party how the session is going for them. Is it helping or not? If not, what can be done to make it more effective? It may be possible to do this in the joint meeting, or it may merit the face-saving privacy of a one-to-one (caucus), before returning to negotiations on details. Unless surfaced, such conscious or often unconscious behaviour 'drivers' may well sabotage any progress through the processual mediation stages towards a settlement.

- Consider the implications of gender balance when co-working, perhaps as a result of indicators picked up in the individual pre-mediation assessment meetings. Where mediator availability prevents a mixed-gender partnership, then at least acknowledge it at the start of the joint meeting, for example by saying something along the lines of 'Obviously there are three women in the room and one man, so if that becomes a problem for either of you please say.' Similar sensitivity and overt acknowledgement also applies to a female or male mediator working solo with a couple made up of a man and a woman.

- Monitor the gender style preferences actively. Co-mediation may well help to balance such issues. It can bring the opportunity for the mediator who is not directly engaged in the nitty-gritty negotiations to observe and comment on the interpersonal communication interactions. See more on this in Chapter 6 on mediation process flexibility and co-working.

- Comment on what you are observing with the parties. Often in mediation, the most helpful and effective thing to say and comment on is simply what is in your own head, framing it as a question. If your hypothesis is not affirmed by them, nothing will have been lost. If, on the other hand, one or both affirm it, then the issue is out in the open and can be explored in terms of how to manage it effectively.

- Question why someone is leaving the room unexpectedly. When a client walks out from a session, consider to what extent it may have had to do with diversity of thinking and communication styles between mediator(s) and client(s). When one party walks out it is often a result of the practitioner failing to spot the warning signals leading up to the action. Typically these signals include a rise in verbal and emotional 'temperature', moving forward on their seat, reaching for their bag, etc. If the client leaves the room, they will effectively have taken control of the mediation process. The experienced practitioner will read the signs, comment on what they observe, propose a break and move the parties to separate rooms. They should then discuss with each party whether and how to proceed. Often they will agree to reconvene, if necessary with some ground rules on behaviour. Alternatively, they may agree to make another appointment, or withdraw from mediation, temporarily or completely. A mediation breakdown should always be an issue to take to supervision, as a mature professional reflective learning exploration. For example questioning, in the heat of the moment, perhaps due to high conflict and emotion, did I/we miss something, maybe something connected to gender communication difference?

Some conclusions

The above discourse is designed to raise awareness and debate on the topic of gender difference and diversity.

In day-to-day practice, it may not feature particularly highly on the scale of issues that challenge our competence as mediators. Nor may it arise as a problem for the majority of our clients. Nevertheless, it does connect with a range of potential difficulties, which may be overlooked in the context of ever-increasing pressure on practitioners, for example, to process more and more referrals, and achieve a faster settlement/agreement rate against a backcloth of ever diminishing resources. The topic also goes to the heart of ideas about how we learn as professionals from reflecting on our practice. As referred to elsewhere in this book, Donald Schön refers to this when he says:

> What is the kind of knowing in which competent practitioners engage? In what sense, if any, is there intellectual rigor in professional practice? I begin with the assumption that competent practitioners usually know more than they can say. They exhibit a

> kind of knowing-in-practice, most of which is tacit. Practitioners themselves often reveal a capacity for reflection on their intuitive knowing in the midst of action and sometimes use this capacity to cope with the unique, uncertain, and conflicted situations of practice. (Schön 1983, p.viii–ix)

Despite workload pressures and resource limitations, from contact with many experienced and competent practitioners, there is hope for a degree of optimism. There is too a growing desire amongst practitioners to push the boundaries of their knowledge, skills and strategies. We must continue to develop, explore and debate such areas of our practice as referred to by Schön as 'tacit'. If indeed we do know more than we say, then let us articulate what it is we know.

Given the initial recognition in this chapter of the controversial nature of this topic, see another writer who states:

> My goal in this book is not to deny that there are any differences between men and women, nor to suggest that people should not be interested in those differences. Rather, my goal is to separate facts from myths, evidence from anecdote and reasonable conclusions from speculative and sweeping generalisations. If we are serious about understanding the relationship between language and gender, we need more sophisticated ways of thinking about men and women, their similarities and differences. (Cameron 2007, pp.20–21)

Cameron's book, *The Myth of Mars and Venus*, makes an important and challenging contribution to the debate. However, I sense that the main thrust of her critical challenge has less to do with accepting that such differences exist but with the danger that they may result in stereotypes. If this happens, such stereotypes can result in perceiving and categorising men and women as more or less suited to certain roles and expectations, for example about positions at work, parenting and leadership, and hence lead to discrimination. Hopefully, this chapter helps to avoid such dangers, given that its primary focus is on raising awareness for mediators and using that understanding to improve practice. It also addresses the practitioners' professional responsibility and accountability for essential fundamental principles, such as equality of opportunity, power balance and safety in the mediation process.

Are we asking the right question regarding gender differences?

Much of the literature on gender difference referred to in this chapter dates back some three decades and typically refers to significantly earlier scientific studies and findings. Consequently, it seemed appropriate that more contemporary studies should be accessed in the hope of finding greater consensus. Online scanning reveals that scientific studies have increased exponentially over time, but so has the controversy. Experienced mediation practitioners have come to understand that the search for truth and facts with disputants is a fool's errand. As stated earlier, clients' idiosyncratic historical accounts of the dispute inevitably include widely differing facts and truths. This may well be so with the ongoing search for facts about gender differences. Consequently, this debate should perhaps be less about whether or not they exist and more about asking a different question. These often highly complex academic issues generally take us no further in the Haynesian 'So what?' question referred to earlier. Brain structure differences and the nature-nurture debate seem in the main to be increasingly acknowledged as fact. It is the cause and effect debate that seems destined to be at the heart of gender communication differences. Given the anecdotal practice evidence of difference, our focus should perhaps not be on the 'if' question, but on awareness and identification of 'how' it should be managed.

References

Borisoff, D. and Victor, D. (1989) *Conflict Management: A Communication Skills Approach*. New Jersey: Prentice Hall.

Cameron, D. (2007) *The Myth of Mars and Venus*. Oxford: Oxford University Press.

Gray, J. (1992) *Men Are from Mars, Women Are from Venus: A Practical Guide for Improving Communication and Getting What You Want in Your Relationships*. London: HarperCollins.

Greenstein, B. (1993) *The Fragile Male*. London: Boxtree Ltd.

Luskin, B.J. (2016) *The Media Psychology Effect. MRIs Reveal Unconscious Bias in the Brain: Shining a Light on an Elephant in the Room*. Psychology Today. Accessed on 14/09/2020 at www.psychologytoday.com/gb/blog/the-media-psychology-effect/201604/mris-reveal-unconscious-bias-in-the-brain

Pease, A. and Pease, B. (1998) *Why Men Don't Listen and Women Can't Read Maps: How We're Different and What to Do About It*. Mona Vale NSW: Pease Training International.

Peterson, B. (2004) *Cultural Intelligence: A Guide to Working with People from Other Cultures*. Boston, MA: Intercultural Press.

Schön, D. (1983) *The Reflective Practitioner: How Professionals Think in Action*. New York: Basic Books.

Tannen, D. (1991) *You Just Don't Understand: Women and Men in Conversation*. London: Virago.

CHAPTER 5

Apology and Reconciliation in Mediation

Such terms as apology and reconciliation are not commonplace in the everyday language of dispute resolution and mediation. Nevertheless, anecdotal evidence from practice suggests that they can have a significant positive benefit for people in conflict. The time may now have come that they can be explored and developed as strategies for contemporary dispute resolution practitioners. Potentially they can be applied across the wide range of dispute contexts, from community, neighbourhood, family, health care, workplace, commercial and indeed worldwide conflicts.

This chapter will define and explore both concepts in terms of their potential place in alternative dispute resolution and mediation. Each will be considered in its own right, rather than with any assumption that they may happen together, or indeed happen at all. They may not occur during the time of the mediation process itself but might come later, perhaps as a result of improved communication as an outcome of the mediation process.

CASE STUDY: The power of apology in family mediation
Roger and Anita had been locked in conflict on a whole range of issues for over six years since they divorced, particularly over contact arrangements. They had come to mediation on the advice of Anita's

solicitor to attempt to resolve their latest problems. Anita said that she wanted to improve the consistency, frequency and reliability of contact between the children and their father. Roger meanwhile described how he was desperately trying to juggle time with his children, serious work pressures as director of a tech company and the imminent arrival of the first child of his new marriage. The mediator, who I was 'live supervising' while not taking an active part in the mediation, had listened carefully to their stories, skilfully demonstrating impartiality and 'listening with understanding', as the characteristically differing historical accounts of adversarial actions between these two adults unfolded.

Anita looked and sounded extremely tense, her whole demeanour and vocal tone was one of barely suppressed fury. She seemed incapable of saying anything without clenched-teeth anger and bitterness. Roger, on the other hand, looked and sounded guilty and defensive. In his communication with the mediator, he presented as 'super reasonable', a manner that seemed only to increase the simmering fury and rage of his ex-wife. The mediator duly made good in-depth individual summaries as a prelude to moving the couple on to the 'issues exploration' stage. Their respective negative accounts of each other's behaviour were skilfully 'mutualised' and 'reframed', demonstrating both what they still had in common and their strong commitment to sorting things out through mediation for their children. The mediator then proposed that this might be a good time to move on to exploring what each of them were hoping to gain from the meeting, but added that she wondered if there was anything else either wanted to say to each other before doing so. What followed indicated that she had perhaps intuitively sensed something about this couple that had, in turn, inspired her question.

After what felt like a very long and contemplative silence, Roger turned to look at Anita and said, in what sounded like a genuinely authentic tone of contrition: 'I just want to say to you how sorry I am for how badly I treated you after we separated; it was very vindictive. I know that I did lots of things to upset and hurt you and that those things upset the children too. I want to apologise for that. I am very sorry. I am not apologising for leaving you, because I still believe that our marriage was at an end. But I am apologising for the way I did it. It was inexcusable; you did not deserve that and neither did the kids.' The visible impact on Anita over the next few minutes was as though a heavy cloud had gradually begun to lift. As if for her the 'lights were coming on again'. She looked surprised, confused and tearful, as though many conflicting thoughts crowded her mind. Again, a very long and heavy silence followed, as all in the room waited and wondered how she would respond. Finally, she turned to face Roger directly for the first time in the meeting and said: 'We have both done many stupid and hurtful things to each other in the past six years.' After another long pause, she added: 'But we do have two wonderful children and perhaps it is now time to try to stop doing such things and to see if we can put things right, for their sake.'

With the help of the mediator, the couple went on to reach an agreement on a new contact schedule. We never heard how well the new arrangements worked out, but they did not ask for a further session. Given the long-standing history of habitual conflict, it would perhaps be naive to suppose that everything would be plain sailing from then on. However, there was a powerful sense that something very special and important happened in the room that day. Not for the first time, as practitioners, we learned something crucial from clients about what they wanted and needed. They provided valuable information on how to further develop our practice as mediators. It also raised questions about how many other clients in mediation might benefit from the emotional release that can come for both the alleged perpetrator and the injured party from such communication.

The historical perspective

Relatively little has been published in mainstream mediation literature on the issues covered in this chapter. Over the last three decades of the development of mediation, these terms generally tended to be regarded as outside of the practitioner's remit. This was in part linked to an early emphasis on the extent to which mediation differed from other activities such as counselling, therapy, welfare and legal advice. During that period practitioners tended to spend more time describing what mediation *was not* and did *not offer* than what it *was* and *could offer*. The primary educational focus on these differences by mediators was mainly directed at politicians, judges and lawyers. With hindsight, this may have accounted for years of ongoing limited understanding of its potential benefits by the general public.

Early influential North American models and styles of practice typically emphasised such concepts as 'future focused', 'time limited' and 'settlement seeking'. They generally discouraged any focus on history or the emotional effects of conflict. The primary aim tended to be described as reaching agreement or 'cutting a deal'. In the process, early practitioners tended to be what can best be described as 'agreement-led'. Anything less than an agreement was likely to be regarded as a failure. Not surprisingly, in the circumstances at that time of early development, a tick on the agreement form was seen as crucial to convincing would-be referrers and bring greater prospects of legal aid funding. It was some years before mediators began to reflect on issues of agreement viability and durability over time. One effect of such reflection began to influence some practitioners to spend time 'reality testing' agreements. This often included exploring with parties what might go wrong with the plans, and therefore what details could be added, so as to limit the chances of breakdown. Anecdotally, those practitioners still wedded to the 'cutting a deal' style were inclined to say: 'No way am I opening that can of worms. If I get a deal, I will run with it; better to stop while you are ahead.' This discussion as to the extent mediation might have a therapeutic outcome – if it has one at all – should not be seen as suggesting that a practitioner should attempt to persuade clients to add it to their agenda. Rather, it was an attempt to raise awareness of disputants' needs and to develop a capacity to 'watch and listen outside of the box' for verbal and non-verbal signals. In his excellent book *Embodied Conflict: The Neural Basis of Conflict and Communication,* Tim Hicks, in a section on 'Recovery from Betrayal or Injury', writes:

> It is often the case that there has been betrayal and/or some level of injury in a conflict, whether the injury be economic, physical, psychological or social. In these cases, to resolve the conflict, the consequences of betrayal must often be addressed, one way or another. (Hicks 2018, p.96)

> The apology creates a shared reality of knowing and meaning. In these ways, apologies provide a kind of soothing and can be part of the healing process. (Hicks 2018, p.97)

The author also usefully explores and extends developments in neuroscience in the understanding of how the areas of the brain that register physical pain are the same centres that are activated by emotional pain.

Apology explored

From experience of running many training workshops on facilitating apology, and from the limited range of literature on the topic, it becomes clear that apology is a very complex business. Each of us will have our own highly idiosyncratic values and opinions on the issue. Such differences need to be understood and respected if as practitioners we were to consider exploring it with parties in dispute.

The Oxford English Dictionary, as quoted in Schneider (2000), defines an apology as: 'to acknowledge and express regret for a fault without defence'. These last two words 'without defence' can be seen to feature substantively in the key elements of a genuine apology. Schneider (2000) explores apologies in relation to mediation and comments:

> Apology, however, is clearly not about problem-solving. Nor is it about negotiation. It is, rather, a form of *ritual* exchange where words are spoken that may enable closure. There is often a felt

need for some acknowledgement of the harm done, a need for some acceptance of personal responsibility for the injury inflicted, in short, an apology. (Schneider 2000, p.1)

In the above case example, Roger seemed to meet all of those three key elements.

Some mediator strategies

Unlike the case referred to above, some would-be apology conversations may need help from the mediator. The person contemplating the possibility of giving an apology may have concerns. For example: Will they be able to find the right words? Will their apology be rejected so that they lose face? Will it be used against them in the negotiations and/or the final settlement? Will it be reciprocated, where they believe that the other side has also offended against them? For the 'injured party' the concerns might include: Are they prepared to consider fully accepting an apology? Would it help them and/or their situation? Is the time right, or are their emotions still too raw? How will they know it is really meant and not just a trick to get the other off the hook? Will it mean that what happened and all the hurt that they felt did not matter?

For some clients, these issues might be possible to explore in a joint session. However, it may be that one or more individual caucus (one-to-one) meetings with the mediator may be required to provide greater face-saving security and informed choice for each party. For example, a caucus could provide the opportunity to review some of the questions referred to above for the alleged perpetrator and victim. It might also be necessary to consider just what it was that was being apologised for and why. For example, Roger was quite specific that he was not apologising for ending the marriage but rather for how he had gone about it.

The actions of the mediator are complex in terms of the fundamental principles that govern their professional role behaviour. Mediator practitioners are governed by their regulatory bodies such as the Family Mediation Council (FMC) which is defined in a very detailed 'Code of Practice'. One particularly key example of a fundamental principle is listed under the section 'Conduct of Mediation'. Here, the importance of such principles as 'impartiality' and 'neutrality' are endorsed in paragraph 6 as: 'Mediators must assist participants to define the issues, identify areas of agreement, clarify areas of disagreement, explore the options and seek to reach agreement upon them.' This is highlighted particularly here because it goes to the heart of frequent debates about 'facilitative' versus 'directive' models of practice. Basically, this element of the code makes it clear that it is for the clients, not the mediator, to define the agenda for negotiations between them. This underscores the notion that the issues in dispute are the private domain of the parties and, as such, the latter should be regarded as the 'experts'. This expertise includes not just understanding them but also being best placed to resolve them together, with the non-directive support of the practitioner. For members of the College of Mediators, these issues are clearly described in the latest Code of Practice 2017 and are summarised here insofar that they link to specifics of our discourse:

2 AIMS AND OBJECTIVES

2.1 Mediation aims to assist participants to reach decisions which they consider appropriate to their own particular circumstances.

2.2 Mediation also aims to assist participants to communicate with one another now and in the future and to reduce the scope or intensity of the dispute or conflict.

2.3 Mediators should have regard to the ethics of mediation in that it should be carried out in a way that seeks to:

- provide a full opportunity for participants to express their views and concerns about the dispute, and at the same time

- minimise distress to the participants and any others involved
- promote as good a relationship between the participants and any others involved as possible
- recognise and manage the risk of abuse to any of the participants or others involved
- reduce conflict and misunderstanding
- be clear and open about the financial cost to the participants
- enable the participants to reach a mutually agreed outcome

4.7 Children and Young People

4.7.1 Where decisions made in mediation have an impact on children and young people, mediators have a special concern for their welfare. They must encourage participants to focus upon the needs of the children and must explore the situation from the child's point of view.

As a consequence of these very appropriate ethical principles, the key issue here relates to the extent to which practitioners facilitate the process of disputants' agenda development and not if but how they do that.

Potential implications for practice

Given some of the complexities referred to above, why indeed would a mediator 'go there'? A significant number of mediation referrals will likely include people for whom 'getting on with life' is contingent on what Schneider calls 'repair work' and 'closure'. He goes on to say: 'Divorce mediation offers just such an opportunity for clients to acknowledge that they have acted in ways that have created injury and are sorry for the damage that they have done to their marriage and their spouse' (Schneider 2000, p.1). Whilst the focus here is on marriage, the same principles could be applied to a wide range of other dispute contexts. Schneider's references to 'injury' and 'damage' are worthy of further consideration, given the significance of this focus on apology. Language and metaphors used by the injured party in mediation such as 'hurt', 'damaged', 'destroyed' and 'wounded' are often as vivid as those used to describe physical harm. Along with Hicks above, another writer comments on this issue as follows:

> When we talk about being dumped or rejected, we use the same vocabulary we'd employ to describe a physical injury. Pain might be nothing more than an apt metaphor for our emotional anguish – after all, there's no mistaking a broken heart for a broken bone. Still, if you ask someone about the worst moments in their life, they might 'reach way back into early childhood and recount an experience of being socially rejected,' says Naomi Eisenberger, a psychologist at UCLA. 'I was just sort of curious as to why this is. Why does it affect us so deeply?' ... The brain seems to process the pain of being separated from or rejected by others 'in a manner that looks very similar to physical pain'. (Wnuk 2018)

Where this potential need for 'emotion-talk' and/or apology might not arise naturally, or not be detected by the mediator, it is possible a significant number of clients may be lost from the mediation process. If efforts to surface a felt need regarding the past and ongoing emotional issues fail, the client may feel that they are in the wrong place and/or at the wrong time. Heightened awareness of such issues might well bring the opportunity for mediators to facilitate more of the sorts of discourse that was so impressively managed by Roger and Anita.

Possible indicators of need and some useful questions for the practitioner

Judging by responses at training workshops, there is an increasingly strong interest across the whole range of mediation contexts and the potential for facilitating constructive emotion and apology.

It is possible to define a list of potential 'needs-indicators', based on observations of clients' behaviour. For example:

- Despite several meetings and some brief movement in negotiations, unexpressed underlying emotion in one or both clients continue to result in 'stuckness' or 'impasse'.

- Despite initial individual assessment meetings, little or no significant level of emotion is expressed over time. There may be a sense that one or other disputant is tiptoeing around some 'masked' conflict. This may be out of fear that if exposed, it might not be managed constructively.

- Despite initial screening for safety, one party may be intimidated or under threat from the other to avoid reference to certain issues. It is not uncommon for non-verbal evidence of this to fail to be noticed by a practitioner, who may be concentrating on the detail and factual matters of negotiations. For example, it may be a particular look or tone of voice that is well understood by a target of intimidation or abuse.

- There may quite simply be a lack of 'conflict energy' between the parties for movement in the change process. I gave a family mediation example of this in my first book:

> With some couples, a wish to avoid any acrimony can protract the negotiation of practical arrangements for separation. It is as if they are working so hard to be civilised and non-adversarial that they fail to generate sufficient heat to create the split. One such couple repeatedly asserted 'peace, calm and love at all costs' despite their strong assertions that the marriage was over. As a consequence, their efforts to organise the details of contact arrangements became so drawn out as to extend some 18 months and some dozen or so sessions

of mediation. What eventually caused a seismic shift of energy, in this case, was that one of them found and moved in with a new partner. The turmoil resulting from a third party becoming involved directly in the lives of the children was all that was needed to generate enough conflict energy to confirm more definitely the death of the marriage and need for real change. (Whatling 2012, p.138)

Experience from practice shows that a potential 'apology seeker' may not use the word 'apology' or 'apologise'. They may not even be consciously aware that an apology is what they seek. Instead, they may say things like: 'The other person has never understood, acknowledged or realised how hurtful they were or how much pain they caused.' This important difference underlines the need for practitioners to raise their awareness and respond with appropriate open questions. It is also possible to produce a potential list of model questions that mediators might use to enquire into the potential for emotional discourse and/or apology when perhaps they sense that an apology seems to be waiting in the wings for a cue to come on stage. In the joint session, examples might be:

- 'Sometimes when people are caught up in a dispute and conflict, the reasons behind it can go on being very upsetting and painful for those involved. When that happens, it can make it hard for one person or the other to put it behind them and move on. How far would you say that might be happening here?' Here the question has deliberately been left open-ended so that either party is free to respond rather than directing it at the perceived victim. Even if the latter is reluctant to respond, the perceived perpetrator might be inclined to engage in a discussion on the issue.

- 'Sometimes when I listen to how you talk together about what has happened, I get a feeling that one or both of you are still perhaps upset or hurt, and that makes it hard to move on. Have I heard that right or not?' If the response suggests that the hypothesis is unconfirmed, then nothing is lost. Conversely, if it is confirmed, then a whole series of other questions can flow from there. For example: 'How far have you been able to talk about what happened? Sometimes when there is so much to deal with and arrangements needing to be put in place it can be hard to talk about what led up to being here and all the emotions involved. If you were willing to take some time to do that, what would your concerns be as to how that might go?'

- 'Sometimes when I hear you talking together, I get the feeling that there is still some sadness and regret for individual actions that brought you to mediation, and how that affected the other. Have I sensed that correctly or not?' Again, as with the previous example, the response is likely to either shut the discussion down or open it up for more questions about concerns if such issues were explored in a joint session.

For more detail of the range of question styles and examples, see Whatling (2012), Chapter 4, 'Questioning Skills'.

To return to the previous case example, what Roger had decided to do was to say what he wanted to say to Anita and to take the risk that it might be rejected or be thrown back in his face. What he said in his own words is also graphically expressed by the words of Carl Schneider: 'An apology is often a means of saying, Yes, there has been a terrible wound here, for which I am truly sorry. My intention is not to destroy you. I am ending this marriage, but I would like to close that door gently, not slam it shut' (Schneider 2000, p.1).

Finally, there is one golden rule that may determine the extent to which an apology is accepted or rejected. The rule is very simple, but so many apologists fail to understand the principle behind it, and hence the apology is fundamentally flawed. The error stems from the two-letter word 'if' that should instead be a four-letter word – 'that'. For example, to say 'I am sorry *if* I offended you', when someone has said clearly that they have been offended by something done or said, is to completely negate the feelings of the offended party.

An interesting issue occurred at a training event in India involving a presentation to a group of supreme court judges. During the subsequent plenary, a judge asked how mediators are trained to be able to assess the genuineness and validity of an apology. My response was that it was not for the mediator to make such a judgement. Whatever the practitioner's personal opinion is as to genuineness, only the receiver has the right to decide its truth or acceptability. With Roger and Anita, my perception, and that of the mediator, was that he looked and sounded genuine, but only Anita had the right to decide. This was also an interesting reminder of how, unlike mediators, lawyers and judges are trained to and spend their day assessing and ruling on matters of what *they* decide are facts and truth.

Reconciliation

The case of Anita and Roger is also useful insofar as it illustrates the extent of the range of a reconciliation outcome from mediation. Given the time span since separation and divorce, marital reconciliation was unlikely to happen. However, what did appear to happen was the start of a restoration of constructive communication and a potential reconciliation of their capacity for parental responsibility and focus on the needs of their children.

Over the years of development of family mediation, as with apology, the word reconciliation had been largely absent from the vocabulary of practitioners. During the mediation information and assessment meeting (MIAM), mediators should be asking questions about the extent to which each party considered the spousal relationship to be at an end. If one or another responded with any doubt, they could be invited to consider raising that as an issue for the joint meeting agenda. Assuming both parties believed that the relationship was definitely at an end, it is unlikely that practitioners will raise the idea of reconciliation again. Anecdotal evidence from observers of the MIAM suggests that the extent to which reconciliation is referred to at all by mediators is very varied. One potential client reported that on approaching a mediation service and asking if reconciliation could be discussed they were told that it could not. Allegedly the service held the view that clients wanting mediation would both have decided that the relationship was at an end. Mediation would, therefore, focus on the negotiations for the necessary settlement.

The first UK College of Family Mediators Code of Practice listed examples of potentially valid agenda issues which included the extent to which the marriage or spousal relationship is at an end. The loss of that specific item and list resulted from the redrafting of the College of Mediators Code of Practice to incorporate the wider range of other mediation contexts. The majority of family mediation practitioners would hopefully still support the principle that discussion as to the extent to which the relationship was at an end is an appropriate issue for the agenda. Indeed, a similar potential agenda item might be just as appropriate in other contexts, such as community, workplace, victim-offender or health care complaints mediation, for example the extent that disputants may wish to consider the potential for reconciliation of the previously good neighbour, workplace or doctor-patient relationship.

Extending the above ideas for practitioners

The following quotation very usefully supports the case for exploration of other potential key issues in dispute resolution practice:

> The academic literature on conflict contains little mention of what happens after a conflict episode is regarded as 'over', although the assumption is that each conflict episode within a relationship

> is affected by previous episodes and will, in turn, affect future ones. Whether a particular episode is productive or destructive will affect how the next episode unfolds. Various researchers have shown that conflict within a relationship can evolve into competitive escalation or avoidance cycles. The goals, therefore, in teaching people how to manage conflict are generally geared towards teaching them. (Lulofs and Cahn 2000)

The writers go on to highlight the potential value in helping clients understand how to manage disputes to prevent their escalation. Additionally, they can be helped in expressing emotions constructively, negotiating and enhancing their future relationships by constructive conflict resolution.

The text is taken from a particularly valuable book, *Conflict: From Theory to Action*, which includes a chapter, 'After the Conflict: Forgiveness and Reconciliation'. It is important to recognise that this is an academic work, rather than written from the mediation practice context. Consequently, reference to 'teaching people how to manage conflict' needs, for mediation practitioners, to be translated in terms of 'facilitation by informed party consent', rather than any didactic or pedagogical activity.

Little has been written about one important potential serendipitous outcome from mediation. Having been through the process, the parties may have learned something about how to manage future conflicts themselves. If not, they may at least be more inclined to return to mediation before allowing future disputes to escalate out of control.

Further exploration of the potential for reconciliation in dispute resolution

Through enquiring about each party's view about the end of a previously good relationship, the practitioner can explore possibilities for reconciliation in mediation. In the case of family mediation, they might inquire as to any need for reconciliation of their role as parents so as to focus on the best interests and needs of their children. Another reconciliation issue might focus on how far each party wished to explore the potential for maintaining positive links with extended family and friendship networks. Separation and divorce frequently result in side-taking by extended family members and friends, sometimes referred to as the 'Greek chorus'. Commonly this may fracture relationships, often with long-term loss and negative effects, particularly for the children. It may be that valuable work can be done during mediation on how to manage the Greek chorus to attempt to limit collateral damage. This applies in all dispute resolution contexts, for example workplace and neighbour contexts. For some people, disputes may also involve issues regarding the reconciliation of each client within their faith and/or social community. Substantial personal experience of working with different cultures and faith groups has demonstrated how, in the conflict between the parents and large close-knit extended family, at least one parent may withdraw from traditional prayer and community centre social events. If this happens, it may well be experienced by other community members, the extended family and faith leaders as a matter of great shame. The sense of shame comes from a deeply rooted regard for the welfare of all community members and therefore a sense that they may have failed to help the family to stay connected in a way that saved face.

The above discussion has extended the potential range of reconciliation contexts beyond that of simply a focus on the spousal relationship. It also raises awareness of important faith and cultural issues, in a way that members of non-Western communitarian cultural and faith communities may find reassuring when considering mediation. How often do the current generation of Western practitioners understand and enquire about such reconciliation matters across the range I have identified? If they do not, there may be a strong case for adding such questions to their repertoire. If they do, then there is a need to ensure that such enquiries fit ethically with principles regarding clients' rights to identify and determine issues for the agenda. Mediators also need to monitor the extent to which such questions flow from genuine professional curiosity and are consistent with professional codes of practice and are not 'cross-wired' to any personal assumptions regarding faith and cultural values. I have referred to this issue in Chapter 1, 'Transitions'.

For further, more detailed discussion on these potentially challenging ethical matters, see Chapter 8, 'Mediating High Conflict Matters'.

How family mediation differs from other dispute contexts

In dispute resolution practice between two or more people and across the spectrum of contexts, differing levels of relationship between the disputants will be influenced by the closeness of emotional relationships. For example, in a workplace dispute, at one level, the parties have shared close proximity at an office and this perhaps includes out-of-office social events. By comparison, a large company dispute with a staff group may include people who rarely, if at all, meet face to face. By comparison, it is useful to compare that context with family disputes since contextual emotions and disputant behaviour are likely to differ substantially from most other contexts. During the courtship phase leading up to the decision to form a spousal relationship and/or marriage, a series of complex discussions and negotiations will take place regarding the potential emotional, psychological and sociological terms of the relationship 'contract'. At the heart of this elaborate ritual is the process of both hitherto separate people redefining themselves from an 'I' identity to a 'we' construct. Conversations will progressively be reconfigured from individual identity statements about the minutiae of likes, dislikes, politics, values, accommodation, holidays, food, music, etc. These relational explorations rarely require an absolute consensus on any particular detail and yet are likely to need the suggestion of a 'good enough' foundation to offer the potential viability of a more intimate partnership than the 'just good friends' concept. In other words, the ritual results in a merging of their perceptions of the world, in which the past, the present and the future form a framework of new shared meaning. It needs to be understood that having reached a 'good enough' conjoining level the process is not finalised but will continue over time as each progresses and changes through new life circumstances and challenges. A key feature of the strength and durability of the relationship often stands or falls by each partner's capacity to accept and adapt to changes in the other. Another key feature of this shared meaning I/we ritual includes the creation of what might be called 'trust bonds'. These bonds involve a range of mutual contractual understandings, regarding such matters as fidelity in intimate relationships, financial security, parenting and child safeguarding, extended family relationships, etc. These bonds are the essential ingredients or 'glue' that binds the qualitative security and dependability of the partnership. Where either partner is found to have broken one of those leading to separation, for example the fidelity bond, a common reaction of the other partner is to adopt a position of 'all bets are off'. The alleged 'guilty' partner is frequently described as 'amoral' and ergo 'unfit' or unsafe to be trusted across the whole range of trust bonds, including parenting and the protection of children and financial assets. Social friendships and extended family relationships are commonly drawn into the dispute and frequently result in side-taking, which all too often poses potentially serious effects on the well-being of children. Where a relationship separation results, it may take several years for each party to recover. Not only does each face the mourning of the loss of the relationship with all its past and future aspirations but also the complexity of reversing the process of defining themselves as the 'we' and back to the 'I'. This process also has to include dealing with their sense of self-esteem and self-image that is damaged for their part in the relationship breakdown and any guilt or shame effects alleged by the former partner. Even if they accepted just

50 pr cent of the 'blame' that is still likely to make it difficult to accept internally and psychologically. As a consequence they will tend to displace most or all of the blame onto the other party, often expressed as 'I know I was not the ideal partner but that was nothing compared to the things they did and that I had to live with'.

In mediation, the experienced practitioner will be well accustomed to high levels of emotion and conflict. Typically, such behaviour demonstrates that conflict is at its highest, and, conversely, trust is at its lowest. Practitioner skills and strategies will be focused on helping the couple to begin a process of reversing these polarities. In the process, mediation will be facilitating a shift from a spousal to parental communication based on the needs of the whole family. In that delicate process, the 'all bets are off' parent will slowly begin to comprehend that a shattered fidelity bond should not be assumed to have put all other bonds at risk.

CASE STUDY: Apology by proxy

Sue and Steve were attempting to negotiate a financial and child contact agreement. After three meetings it became apparent that Sue was still very hurt, upset and angry that Steve had an affair with one of her friends, although this issue was not on the agenda. Only as each session came close to potential agreement did she express significant anger and reference to his 'adultery'. At such moments Steve's reaction was one of apparent shame and guilt, and he would respond with efforts to apologise to her. The problem was that he would say things like: 'OK, if you want me to apologise I will.' She would respond with something like: 'It is not to do with what I want, it's to do with you meaning what you say.'

The sessions began to go from bad to worse every time this issue flared up again. I decided to see each of them separately. Starting with Sue, I reviewed with her what I had noticed about her feelings and used open questions to clarify her underlying wants and needs. We also reviewed what her problems were with accepting an apology from Steve. Not surprisingly, she feared he would just say it to get himself 'off the hook' and get to a settlement. With Steve, I commented on my observation of his attempts to apologise. He acknowledged that he had always been less able to express his feelings than Sue. I suggested that he tried to say to me what he had been trying to say to Sue. After a couple of not very convincing attempts, he relaxed and gave what sounded to me like a very genuine and convincing apology. Back in the joint session, I invited Steve to say to Sue what he wanted to say by way of apology. Sadly, whilst trying his best he again got it wrong every time. As a consequence Sue responded with a rebuttal of each, as she had done with his previous attempts. At this point, I summarised for each of them what I was observing and commented that in caucus Steve had tried saying what he would like to say to Sue. I wondered if it might help if I said to her what he had said to me. With the agreement of both, I did that, and Sue was visibly moved by this proxy option. After a lengthy silence, Sue said that she now believed it was genuine and that he did mean it. With a note of humour, she added that he had always suffered from 'foot and mouth disease'; namely, when he opened his mouth he tended to put his foot in it. We went on to complete their draft plans for settlement.

This case study illustrates the complexities for both the giver and the receiver despite genuine intentions. This includes finding the right words, using the right tone of voice and adopting the appropriate non-verbal reinforcers, such as eye contact and open posture. There are also important cultural factors related to differing levels of status and face saving, as covered in more detail in Chapter 3. In certain non-Western cultures such as Japan, a neutral proxy apologiser delivering the apology may well be acceptable, since it allows the giver and receiver to save face, compared to a face-to-face experience. Similarly, in all cultures, in civil, commercial, community and workplace contexts, particularly involving different status disputants, a proxy process may have similar benefits. In all such contexts, this proxy option may be appropriate to explore with each disputant where an apology option is being explored. In other words, the 'how' of delivery may be just as important as the 'if'. These issues are also featured in another case example.

CASE STUDY: The 'alpha male' consultant – a health complaint

The case involved a complaint by a patient, Jo, to a hospital trust against a senior consultant surgeon, Nick. Jo had been scheduled for gynaecology day surgery. Nick was well known within the hospital and the complaints team for being verbally aggressive and disinclined to be conciliatory. The hospital chief executive explained the background details to the mediator. He was surprisingly critical of Nick for his general aggressive manner and volatile communication style. Jo, on the other hand, was described as intelligent, but not very articulate, and easily intimidated. The main concern was that unless the matter could be resolved via conciliation, the hospital trust would very likely become embroiled in a lengthy, time-consuming and costly series of complaints tribunal hearings. A case file was provided, which contained several abusive hospital notes from Nick about Jo. It was hard to comprehend that, whatever he may say verbally, he would write such views for a file record, not least since the matter might go to tribunal.

The complaint related to the fact that Jo's boyfriend, Alan, was in prison for a non-violent crime. Given her high anxiety about surgery, it had been agreed that he could be with her in hospital if accompanied by a prison officer. The prison responded well and agreed to the arrangements. On the day of surgery, Jo was in bed and Alan with the officer. Alan, wearing handcuffs discreetly covered by a coat, was sitting with her. The ward sister appeared and declared that the hospital policy allowed for only one friend to be at the bedside. Regardless of the explanations given, the sister maintained her position, and, when contacted, Nick supported her and cancelled the day surgery. He also decided that, because Jo was likely to become hysterical again, she would now have to come in for an overnight admission and Alan could not be with her. Jo agreed to be visited at home for an initial mediation assessment. The surgery had been successful, but she was still very emotional and upset about the day surgery incident. Her fears about conciliation were that Nick would not listen to her or understand how she had felt about the incident. Additionally, she wanted to think that hospital policy could be changed so that other people would not have to go through the same experience in the future. Talking through her thoughts about a joint meeting, she was anxious about going to the hospital again and that Nick would react with aggression as he had previously. Other venue options were explored, and it was agreed that her GP surgery would be a more comfortable option.

At a solo assessment meeting with Nick, he arrived late, stating he could only spare ten minutes as he had a heavy workload to attend to. After reviewing his perception of the history, he was asked what he thought would happen if a joint meeting was arranged with Jo. He responded that he would probably tell her what a stupid and selfish bitch she was, after all he had done to treat her medical condition. He added that he would always 'tell it like it is'. When asked what effect he thought that might have on attempts to resolve the complaint, he relaxed, laughed and said he knew it would probably make things far worse. He was advised that a joint meeting would not be arranged if that was the likely outcome and that the situation would in all probability result in time-consuming tribunal meetings. Surprisingly, he then said he was prepared to apologise to Jo for what had happened that day and for reacting so angrily. Even more surprisingly, he said that since the incident, he had completely rewritten the hospital policy procedures for prisoners to attend with a partner or next of kin and that a police or prison officer could also attend. He then gave consent for a copy of the new policy document to be given to Jo, together with his readiness to apologise. Despite the file records and aggressive communications thus far, he did seem genuine in his wish to put things right. He was also willing to attend a joint meeting with Jo at the GP clinic. When this was all fed back to Jo, she was surprised and impressed, both with his readiness to apologise and with the new protocol. Since both actions had met her primary hopes for conciliation, she was satisfied with the outcome and did not think they needed to meet face to face. All outcome details were duly summarised in writing for Jo, Nick and the hospital chief executive. This case is a useful reminder of how important it is for practitioners not to be too alarmed at the presenting positions and threats made by people in dispute and the importance of demonstrating impartiality and of facilitating a needs-led dialogue.

The case also usefully illustrates the potential benefits of saying sorry, and of taking a non-defensive reaction to complaints. Following the publication of the government report 'Being Heard' (Wilson 1994), I started delivering training workshops for hospital trusts on complaints conciliation. Complaints conciliators, at that time largely unpaid volunteers, were appointed to hospital complaints departments. They were frequently advised by the complaints officer to work with patients to encourage them to withdraw the complaint. I was subsequently appointed as a practice consultant to the London boroughs complaints consortium. A London regional complaints survey (unpublished) found that, despite the fears of GPs and hospital trusts, at the top of the list of patients' and relatives' hopes from making a complaint were: to be listened to and understood by health care professionals; to understand what had happened where treatment had failed; to help health professionals learn from mistakes so that future patients could receive better outcomes; where possible, to restore a previously good patient-doctor relationship; and where appropriate an apology. Interestingly, some 70 per cent of complaints were to do with doctor-patient communication, for example rudeness, not listening or rushing a consultation, rather than clinical treatment matters.

Finally, whilst space limits detail on potential litigation implications of giving an apology, it is worth noting the increasing international developments on this issue. Despite the reputation of the USA having a highly litigious compensation culture, an increasing number of states are passing laws that prohibit an apology being brought as evidence of guilt in any subsequent court proceedings. For example:

> Since 1986, apology legislation has been introduced in 56 jurisdictions, including the United States, Australia, Canada, England and Wales, and a Private Member's Bill has been tabled in the Scottish Parliament. More recently, in June 2015, a Consultation Paper on the Enactment of Apology Legislation in Hong Kong (the 'Consultation Paper') has been released and public consultation is underway to seek views on whether to enact apology legislation in Hong Kong. Given the growing number of jurisdictions in which apology legislation applies, practitioners involved in international dispute resolution need to understand the rationale and operation of this type of legislation. While the scope of apology legislation varies between jurisdictions there has been a discernible trend towards the adoption of apology legislation that provides: 1. broader legal protection than just the inadmissibility of an apology as evidence of fault or liability; and 2. wider coverage in terms of the types of proceedings covered. Consequently, practitioners involved in international dispute resolution should be conversant with the different apology legislation in operation and how it may affect their cases or clients. (Carroll et al. 2015, p.116)

This chapter has brought together important topics and potential practice developments that have hitherto received very limited attention in the field of dispute resolution and mediation literature. Recent anecdotal evidence suggests a significant rise in high conflict and emotion between parties attending mediation. At seminars, workshops and during supervision, practitioners increasingly express concern about such developments. They ask for more ideas and training in how best to manage such contemporary conflict patterns. Of particular concern, some mediators are considering whether, if such high conflict and emotion indicators are detected during the initial assessment stage, disputants should be not be offered mediation. As referred to above, such conflict developments and ideas for different session management options are covered in more detail in Chapter 8, 'Mediating High Conflict Matters'. Also as referred to earlier, there is a risk that if potential high emotion is not identified or managed effectively, one or both parties may leave the process. People seeking help from a range of professionals tend to look for signs in the practitioner's behaviour and questions as a guide to how best to behave as clients. If practitioners fail to enquire about a possible need for such issues to be explored, the client may sense that they are in the wrong setting and leave, often without giving a reason. Sadly, such a withdrawal may be regarded by the practitioner as an indication that such clients were unsuitable, or perhaps not ready, for mediation.

The writer and trainer from the USA John Haynes, who had a substantial influence on early developments in the UK, went so far as to define emotion as 'un-useful dialogue'. Together with his disinclination to spend time on history discourse, and his future-focused and settlement-seeking styles, this became something of a mantra associated with his name. He did explore this in more detail and writes:

> It is useful to think about client emotional behaviour in two ways: offensive and defensive. Offensive behaviour is non-useful and best ignored by the mediator unless it prevents progress in the mediation process. Defensive emotional statements are often useful because they alert the mediator to underlying issues, or indicate emotional issues which, if dealt with, enable the mediator to continue the mediation process, negotiating for a solution that meets the parties' goals. (Haynes 1993, p.11)

I had enormous admiration for John and learned much from his training events in the UK. However, on these issues of history and emotion, I fundamentally disagreed with him. It now seems likely that the time is right for practitioners to raise their awareness of such history discourse and any emotional 'repair needs'. The management of high conflict and emotion has always been the 'bread and butter' of mediator practice. These issues will not go away and indeed will in all probability increase. The chapter is an attempt to identify yet another addition to the mediator's skills and strategies toolbox, enhanced by quality training, supervision and lifelong reflective practice.

References

Carroll, R., To, C. and Unger, M. (2015) Apology Legislation and its Implications for International Dispute Resolution. *Dispute Resolution International 9*, 2, 115–138.
College of Mediators (2017) Code of Practice for Mediators. College of Mediators.
Haynes, J. (1993) *The Fundamentals of Family Mediation*. London: Old Bailey Press.
Hicks, T. (2018) *Embodied Conflict: The Neural Basis of Conflict and Communication*. New York: Routledge.
Lulofs, R. and Cahn, D. (2000) *Conflict: From Theory to Action*. Boston: Allyn & Bacon.
Schneider, C. (2000) What It Means to Be Sorry: The Power of Apology in Mediation. *Mediation Quarterly 17*, 3.
Whatling, T. (2012) *Mediation Skills and Strategies: A Practical Guide*. London: Jessica Kingsley Publishers.
Wilson, A. (1994) *Being Heard: The Report of a Review Committee on NHS Complaint Procedures*. London: Department of Health.
Wnuk, A. (2018) *Do Hurt Feelings Actually Hurt?* BrainFacts. Accessed on 04/11/2020 at www.brainfacts.org/thinking-sensing-and-behaving/emotions-stress-and-anxiety/2018/do-hurt-feelings-actually-hurt-010518

CHAPTER 6

How Mediators Do What They Do

Exploring a Range of Process Options for Practitioners in Mediation Practice

This chapter will address a number of topics related to the options available to mediators for managing sessions in a way that is best suited to the bespoke needs of their clients. Most of these options will be familiar to trained and experienced practitioners. However, practitioners may have developed them somewhat idiosyncratically from limited knowledge gained in core training or from what commonly used to be described as 'sitting-with-Nellie', which is defined by the Oxford Dictionary of Human Resource Management as 'a term used to describe poor-quality on-the-job training where a trainee is not instructed by a qualified trainer but instead is expected to learn how to do the job by observing someone who has been doing the job for years (i.e. Nellie)'.

For the novice mediator, there can be much to be gained by this historical apprentice learning model. However, the model does assume that Nellie is a skilled practitioner. If in this traditional learning process they had learned appropriate, up-to-date skills, all may be well. If, however, they did not, the outcome may have been a less than ideal learning process. This chapter will also explore the detailed process management of the options or methods for supervising the work of a practitioner. As such, that could be of value to trainee and novice practitioners. It may also be of interest to the more experienced, who may benefit from reviewing how they have evolved their own style over time.

Co-mediation

The co-mediation model is usefully summarised by one writer as:

> This occurs when two mediators, ideally one male and one female, mediate together in a particular case. Co-mediation by two members of the same sex should ideally be avoided because of the risk of perceived bias, and of one of the parties being outnumbered three to one by the opposite sex. Although co-mediation may appear to be more expensive and requires careful planning and time for preparation, there are distinct advantages in using two mediators in certain cases – for example, where there are a number of parties, where additional or complementary expertise may be needed, where there is high conflict or there are particularly difficult circumstances. (Roberts 2014, p.161)

The writer goes on to offer more useful detail on the advantages and potential disadvantages of the model. Her reference to gender balance is also important to communication styles, and difference, as covered in more detail in Chapter 4, 'Gender Difference in Thinking and Communicating and Implications for Mediation Practice'.

Historical developments in co-working

In the early years of the development of mediation in the UK, co-working was without doubt of substantial benefit to novice mediators making the transition from other professional roles (see more details on this in Chapter 1, 'Transitions'). It enabled practitioners to support each other in the relatively uncharted waters of theory and practice, especially in cases of high conflict.

With luck, the colleague would be able to step in supportively, in keeping with the old adage that 'two minds are greater than one'. A further benefit was that co-workers could de-brief on the case and their performance, individually and jointly. The temptation was to devote this time to discuss the clients and case dynamics, but the professionally higher-level and a more difficult activity was that of giving each other constructive critical feedback. As referred to in Chapter 2, 'Supervising Mediation Practice', this is best done by commenting first on what the other did that was effective, and then on what they could do differently/more of/less of, etc. An additional benefit of co-working is that each practitioner could play to their individual strengths in a way that synchronised skills to the benefit of the clients.

One risk here was that to continue to work in that style might mean that neither practitioner learned how to increase their competence in their lesser strengths. Increasingly, good quality trusting partnerships enabled plans for how each could work outside of their comfort zone and develop more strengths across the range in future referrals. In this evolutionary transition from co-working to sole practice, there are strong similarities with early developments of family therapy in the UK and the USA. Over time, in family therapy and mediation, people developed sufficient competence and confidence to work increasingly as sole practitioners. Not only was this economically advantageous but it also simplified the complexities of working well in harmony as co-workers. By way of example, this could be compared with the synchronicity required to play tennis doubles. Playing singles means not needing to take time to plan how the partnership will work best and not needing to have careful regard for what your partner is about to do in play.

In mediation, co-working can be analysed as a complex set of mathematical equations. Each practitioner must be constantly monitoring the quality of their ongoing rapport with the parties jointly and separately. They must equally be monitoring the relationship of the parties' reactions to the mediators as a pair, and their interventions. Added to this total is the need to observe the intervention qualities to and fro between the co-workers and clients. Finally, the mediators must be evaluating the two-way relationship between themselves. All of the above amounts to a surprisingly large sum total of activity. It can be seen from this that to work solo does remove a significant number of responsibilities from the equation. Obviously, the downside of sole working is that the practitioner must carry all responsibility for the relationship observation with all parties and themselves, in addition to the detail of substantive negotiations. Despite the changes over time, co-working remains a valued option for novice mediators, both in terms of their developing confidence and the best interests of the clients. A quality supervisory and mentoring process can monitor how the novice's growing confidence and competence can increase their share of greater activity in sessions. It can allow for post-session de-briefing feedback, and may also enable written 'witness testimony' for the novice's competency assessment evidence portfolio. It is a matter of regret that, over time, the steady decline in co-working practice has become primarily a matter of cost and resource limitation. Whilst this is understandable, it does potentially risk the focus on a bespoke assessment of the needs of each referral, including risk assessment and safe practice. Current best practice principles include the use of co-working in cases of very high conflict; any history of domestic abuse; child protection issues; power imbalance, including gender communication issues; and multiparty meetings.

A structured co-working model

Apart from addressing potential advantages and disadvantages of co-working, writers on this topic generally provide little if any guidance on the *what* and *how* of managing the process. Generally speaking, practitioners are advised to plan specific roles, for example that one will introduce the session and the other will come in on the next stage, etc. They will also have to consider how the less active partner can intervene, should they spot a need to raise other issues or potential new directions. Despite the reassurance of having a partner to share the stress, trainee and novice mediators frequently struggle with the reality of this balance in role-playing.

One little-known example of developing a more structured process model was usefully defined by Thelma Fisher. There is a limit to how much of the detail from her article can be covered here, but the key information will be summarised. In addition to explaining the potential benefits of co-working and how the Swindon mediation service came to identify the need for such a model, she wrote:

> This article surveys the present state of co-working in the practice of those independent family conciliation services affiliated to the National Family Conciliation Council. It proposes that a model of co-working is needed that is specifically tailored to conciliation practice. ... It develops a theoretical base for this model from the concepts of 'content' and 'process' which it links with the 'underlying' and 'substantive' issues brought up by separating and divorcing couples for resolution. (Fisher 1987, p.367)

Thelma went on to say:

> The original model was that one worker chaired the session and was the key negotiation manager, and is also responsible for the secretarial and administrative functions of writing down any agreements and communicating about them to solicitors. The second worker played a more recessive role, contributing to the stages of exploration and option development and identifying what might be overlooked by the busier chairperson, both in noticing individual reactions of either parent or family member and observing the interactions between all the participants; in other words, a live consultation model in the room. (Fisher 1987, p.368)

The Swindon model brings a useful and clearer role distinction to the co-working partnership. Without this clarity of responsibilities, it can be unclear as to who is primarily 'in the driving seat' at any moment. It also risks a sense of the silent observer looking more passive and creates some uncertainty as to when, and for what reason, they might join in the process. As described above, the model brings more clearly defined role responsibilities to each of the workers and hence less of a sense of a dominant versus passive partnership. The article usefully provides more detail of the developmental journey of learning about the options for how to mediate as practitioners and its complexities.

It also includes a case study that uses a diagrammatic flowchart between the couple's exchanges and respective mediator interventions. As a trainer and practice consultant, I have found it helpful to describe the two roles as 'substantive content manager' (SCM) and 'underlying process observer' (UPO). The role of the first is to be highly focused on the detailed negotiations of each agenda issue and potential options that may eventually build towards a settlement plan and agreement. The UPO, on the other hand, is freed up from that responsibility and able to focus instead on the complexity of the interpersonal interactions between the clients and the SCM. As a metaphor, the sole working mediator, like the plate-spinning juggler, must ensure that all are kept spinning and no plate is dropped. Here, they can rest assured that their co-worker is on hand to step in if they miss a crucial 'spin'. By way of example, it may be that the process observer spots that, despite the effectiveness of their colleague, the conflict temperature is rising. One client may be looking more agitated, perhaps increasingly confused, intimidated, withdrawn or upset and emotional. At that point, the UPO is able to move in to draw attention to their observation. Ideally, the co-workers have an agreed signal for this, perhaps when the UPO moves forward in their chair and/or puts a hand on the arm of the SCM and speaks directly to them. A typical comment might be: 'Before we go any further with the details, I just wanted to say that I notice that [name] is looking a bit upset/angry/confused. Have I got that right? If so, I wonder if it might help to take some time to explore that?' What is happening here is highlighting the difference between substantive/practical matters versus the underlying emotive and psychological dynamics. This may or may not also involve communication-style differences referred to in Chapter 4, 'Gender Difference in Thinking and Communicating and Implications for Mediation Practice'. Assuming that the hypothesis of the UPO is confirmed, steering into the issue and facilitating discussion about it will often free up a potential blockage, and, by agreement, enable a return to the substantive negotiations. Where this happens, the usual rule is that the UPO now assumes the role of the SCM and the other co-worker moves into the UPO role. The benefit of this role transition is that it offers a chance for the former UPO to be more active and for their partner to take a break from the pressure of managing the substantive issues. It also models good negotiation and turn-taking behaviour for the parties in dispute.

Shuttle mediation

Shuttle mediation typically involves the mediator(s) moving back and forth between the parties in separate rooms rather than being face to face in joint meetings. One writer summarises the model as: '"Shuttle mediation" consists of individual mediation meetings held with each party separately, with the mediator moving to and fro between them. This is the model used by ACAS [Advisory, Conciliation and Arbitration Service] conciliators and to a large extent in commercial mediation' (Parkinson 1997, p.80). Another writer highlights the potential disadvantages in family mediation:

> In disputes following a family breakdown, the disadvantages of shuttle mediation outweigh the advantages, except in special circumstances such as illness, extreme stress, or fear of intimidation, where it could (although not necessarily) be of

> value as a prelude to joint negotiation. A vulnerable party may feel safer initially communicating at a distance, but it is fair to say that if the level of conflict is that high, mediation is probably not appropriate anyway. (Roberts 2014, pp.159–160)

The writer goes on to list in some detail the disadvantages. Comparing the process of shuttle, some of Roberts' concerns relate to the difficulty the mediator may have in demonstrating impartiality with a consequential risk of a perceived alliance between mediator and one client by the other. The mediator is essentially managing the negotiations by proxy, a consequence which can deprive the parties of learning how to manage the process themselves with the skilful guidance of the practitioner. This mediator process and content control could also lead to manipulation, particularly in difficult and complex cases, whereby the process of message-taking could subtly include potential settlement options or negotiation deal trading. The open demonstrability and transparency of confidences may create doubts in the minds of disputants as to trustworthiness, and finally it does take longer, with implications for financial resources. Anecdotal experience suggests that shuttle is significantly less successful than joint meetings, and in fact, compared to its traditional model referred to above by Parkinson 24 years ago, ACAS has in recent years moved to a preference for joint meetings:

> What happens during mediation? There are distinct phases in the mediation process, and these are variously described in the literature as a three-, four- or five-stage process. Whichever way it is broken down, the essential elements remain the same. The first stage will deal with the parties separately, while the remaining stages will generally be dealt with during the joint session. There may be a need to separate the parties at various points and speak to them individually if there appears to be an impasse or the mediator feels that one side is unwilling to divulge information which might help to break the deadlock. There are

occasions where shuttle mediation has to be used because parties will not agree to sit in the same room with each other; or because at certain points it is more effective to do so. But the aim is to bring them together eventually. (ACAS 2013, pp.8–9)

In summary, given that so much of effective interpersonal communication is non-verbal and tonal, mediation works best when parties in dispute are able to negotiate directly, face to face. From that, we might suppose that if the parties in dispute cannot at some point do that, the odds of successfully enacting any agreement plans are likely to be unfavourable, particularly when children are involved. In family mediation, mediators work carefully and respectfully to help conflicted couples move gradually from a spousal dispute to constructive parental discourse. This highly complex and gradual transition moves over time from the early stages of conflict being at its highest and trust at its lowest to an inversion of these two extremities. Once each parent experiences being genuinely heard and understood by the practitioner, they will be more enabled to start exploring together the needs of the children. Without that skilfully facilitated transition, progress to a negotiated settlement is unlikely to happen.

Managing the process

Few writers give any significant detail on how to manage the shuttle mediation process, instead defining and describing it, while often including opinions as to its pros and cons. A consequence of this lack of detail may be that practitioners have to manage the process largely using a hit-and-miss approach and a large degree of guesswork. Since strategic interventions are often highly complex, it may help to look at the management of the process in more detail.

Not surprisingly, shuttle mediation usually takes longer than a joint meeting. Compared to a joint meeting of two hours, the shuttle is likely to need at least three. During early individual pre-mediation assessment meetings, the shuttle mediation process, and how it will be managed, should be carefully explained to the parties. There is a significant amount of detail to be covered, and people in stressful circumstance often fail to recall all that was said. Best practice increasingly calls for written copies of the mediation arrangements to be provided to all parties. Consequently, what follows is a potential draft statement for parties to have time to absorb the details, after the initial solo assessment session and before the first appointment. Additional notes will be added in italics – they are not for the clients but for mediators' awareness and knowledge.

1. As you know, following your initial assessment meeting, each of you decided to try shuttle mediation, rather than attend joint meetings. What follows is a list of the key details about how shuttle mediation works as a process.

2. Each of you will have a series of one-to-one meetings with the mediator.

3. As a general rule, everything you say will be regarded as confidential, unless you give the mediator express authority to disclose matters to the other person. The only exception to this confidentiality principle, regarding risk and safety, was explained to you at your first assessment meeting.

4. You will each have time alone while the mediator is with the other person. During that time, it will be important for you to try to keep focused on the matters in hand.

5. As a matter of policy, we ask that you do not arrange to meet or telephone other people during this time since this could complicate and compromise the integrity of the process.

6. Every effort will be made to ensure each of you has approximately equal time, but you need to be prepared for the possibility of a few minutes' variations either way. If for

any reason there is any significant delay we would aim to let you know.

7. The first solo meeting with each of you will begin with a reminder of the key principles and process of mediation, particularly regarding confidentiality. It will usually involve a summary of key facts, history and clarification of the agenda issues for each of you. The meeting will usually be concluded with a summary by the mediator of key issues discussed and clarifying what can or cannot be shared with the other party.

8. Before the mediator moves to the other person, you may be asked to think about some specific matters in the time you are alone. For example, you might be asked to reflect on what has been covered in that meeting; to what extent you felt heard, understood and able to discuss matters of concern to you; and any issues that have not been raised so far. You may find it helpful to make some brief notes on any such issues.

9. Ideally, the meetings will progress through the initial stages to consideration of your options for future changes. If this is the case, you may be asked to list your own potential proposals for options, including what you hope for and might be prepared to offer in return.

10. On the question of what can or cannot be shared between you, the mediator may make a written note of the details to be shared.

11. People in the early stages of the dispute are often inclined to focus on and describe negative perceptions of the other and this is quite natural in the circumstances. For example, they tend to list the other person's faults, what they want them to stop doing and their opinion as to the way forward for the future settlement. It may help all people involved

in the dispute to think about what they do want from the other in future, rather than what they don't want.

Reframing such attributions in terms of what the parties do want from each other in future, rather than what they don't want, leads helpfully towards a future-focused problem-solving discourse. Such reframing must satisfy each party as to its accuracy and validity. In other words, the transformation of language captures the essence and authenticity of their perceptions and feelings, rather than simply imposing the mediator's views or opinions. For example, one party may say of his or her partner: 'They have broken all trust between us. I can no longer rely on their promise to change and any agreement they make here is unlikely to be kept.' The mediator might summarise this as: 'What I am hearing is that, if you are to negotiate constructive future plans and arrangements, you would both need to feel confident that you can trust each other to keep to those agreements. If that is a fair summary, how can we word that in terms of specific future-focused actions or behaviours you would want to request of your partner?' In some respects, the mediator can have more influence and flexibility in shuttle mediation to respectfully challenge, probe and clarify the parties' narratives and positions. For example, each person can be asked to imagine how he or she might feel in the position of the other party; what, with hindsight, he or she might have done differently or not at all; and what his or her worst fears might be if mediation is unable to resolve the issues. During a joint meeting, this may risk a defensive face-saving reaction or questioning of the mediator's impartiality. Gradually and respectfully destabilising each party's sense of conviction about their story and fixed position can be a useful way of helping them move on to future-focused problem-solving negotiations.

Such dialogue is not designed to provide an alternative interpretation favoured by the practitioner, but instead gives the opportunity to look at the situation from another position in the landscape. This must also be done with a level of genuine respect that has been earned by the mediator during the earlier stages of the process. At some point, it may be that things have progressed sufficiently well to present an opportunity for a joint session, even if only for the last few minutes of the appointment. Both parties must be very willing and ready for such a possibility without coercion. If either is unsure and still feels unsafe, it should not happen. If it does happen, it can be a useful opportunity to highlight any progress made thus far. It also provides a reality check of the detail regarding who has agreed to do what, when and how. Such reality testing can also usefully include thoughts about what, if anything, might go wrong with the plans, and hence explore ideas as to how to manage any such problems. Some practitioners are reluctant to 'go there', as they say, fearing that it might threaten or undermine progress. However, at the point where the parties are collaborating on agreements, they are more likely to see the importance of doing everything possible to ensure the workability of the plans. It can also provide an opportunity to check how they prefer the wording of the 'outcome statement' to be drafted, thereby increasing their sense of ownership of the plans. Genuine and respectful comments from the mediator as to the progress they have made thus far, compared to when they first arrived, can also bring a rewarding sense of mutual achievement between them.

12. The mediator will aim to summarise this for each of you, with a particular focus on the needs of others involved, especially any children. Depending on the complexity of the issues, these preliminary stages may take some time, but we believe that it is better to clarify the key issues in some detail before moving to the next meeting. If all is progressing well, it might be possible to consider whether each of you are ready to move on to any potential areas of agreement.

13. When recording any agreed plans, we will take care to be sure that you are both satisfied with the wording and are confident that the plans are workable. We will also be encouraging you both to consider what, if anything, could go wrong with plans and what ideas you have for dealing with such problems should they arise.

14. You will need to be aware that any agreed future plans when recorded are not legally binding and tend to be recorded as a memorandum of understanding. Should you wish for the plans to be made legally binding you would need to take legal advice as to how to do that.

Finally, on this topic, it is very common for people experiencing high levels of emotional distress when seen at the initial solo intake assessment interview to ask if they really do have to be in the same room as the other party. Some practitioners may be inclined to respond by immediately offering a shuttle. Anecdotal supervisory experience shows that, particularly with a novice mediator, this may be an indication of their own discomfort with managing high conflict in joint meetings. In most instances, a better response is to ask the client for information as to why that would be of concern to them. Responses usually describe fears that they or the other party may not be able to control their emotion, distress, anger, etc. and may find it all too intimidating to say what needs to be said. The experienced practitioner would attempt to reassure them that it is the mediator's responsibility to help people to manage their feelings so as to ensure that nobody would be intimidated or too distressed to be able to speak for themselves. This would be made clear at the start of the first joint meeting, and it should be made clear that if the practitioner felt that was happening he or she would call for a break. The parties would also be encouraged to ask for a break if at any stage they were too upset or intimidated. A break, in separate rooms, would give a chance for people to calm down and discuss with the mediator whether they felt safe to return to the joint session. At that point any ground rules on behaviour would need to be agreed, or it would be discussed if indeed they wanted to opt for a period of shuttle. Most clients will find such information sufficiently reassuring to commit to joint sessions. Practitioners should also be alert to the possibility that a client insisting on shuttle may be hoping to exercise greater control and power over negotiations and the other party. That is not to say that any doubts about their motive would mean that it should not be tried, but that the behaviour should be monitored.

CASE STUDY: Inappropriate use of shuttle

One family mediation case involved a mother of five children refusing contact for the father. She explained that she was fearful that he would fail to return the children after contact and that she found him too intimidating to attend a joint meeting. Shuttle was agreed and arrangements made for her to arrive some 15 minutes before the father. Despite being told that children should not be brought to the centre, she brought them together with their maternal grandmother. They were accommodated in the waiting room, while the mother was in a separate ground floor room and the father in a room three floors up. Moving between the parties was not only physically demanding for the mediators, but they also became increasingly concerned about the level of control being exercised by the mother. Whenever any progress towards an agreement settlement seemed possible, she would suddenly increase her demands. Eventually, the mediators explained to her their concerns about the lack of progress and that an agreement through mediation seemed unlikely. At this point, the mother disclosed that the father owed her some £50 for clothes from a catalogue and said that if he would repay the debt, contact could be resumed. Not only would she agree a regular contact arrangement, but also he could take them out to lunch from the centre and return them to her by an agreed time. The father accepted the plan, settled that debt and was happily reunited with the children in the waiting room.

This experience is not unique, and this case is offered simply as an example of what may indicate a misuse of mediation. It does not assume a conscious intent by one party to exercise power over the other. A client's original fears and concerns may be entirely genuine. However, at some point, they may become aware of the benefits of using the mediator(s) to increase settlement demands without having to face the other party.

In another case, a mother consistently refused child contact for the father or to meet face to face on the grounds of the father's intimidation. At the next shuttle session, she reported that she had become so frustrated by the behaviour of the children she had phoned the father to come to the house and 'sort his kids out'. The father duly went to the house, they all enjoyed a family tea and he stayed until the children were settled in bed. Despite this, she continued to insist on shuttle sessions and showed a continuous pattern of using the mediators to increase her settlement demands.

When exploring clients' concerns about being in the same room, it is worth considering other, potentially less time-consuming creative options. For example, while a mediator was working with a high conflict couple, a wife frequently became tearful and unable to articulate her feelings and needs. She was asked about this and what could be done to enable her to carry on with the meeting. She explained that her husband was looking at her in a way that he had used in the past when non-verbally 'putting her down' and intimidating her. She added that it was not about his words, nor his tone of voice; it was simply the look on his face. The husband gave what sounded like a genuine apology and fully acknowledged how he had behaved in the past. However, he added that this facial expression was not intended to do that now, but was instead related to his feeling anxious about the potential loss of the marriage, the marital home, contact with their children and maybe even his job. Interestingly, the wife accepted both his apology and his account of how he felt now. Nevertheless, she was unable to use that new understanding to stop her emotional and psychological reaction to it.

The reader might like to consider at this point how they might have responded. At first sight, it seemed as though the situation might have indicated that shuttle mediation was the best option, despite its limitations addressed above. Summarising both parties' positions, I wondered, given that it was not his words or tone of voice, how she might feel not seeing his expression whilst they talked together. She responded favourably, so I suggested that they just tried a few minutes sitting back to back whilst still able to see me. It worked and they went on to put together a draft interim plan for a settlement, which they later consolidated into a divorce consent order.

Involving significant others in mediation

This section explores the potential advantages and disadvantages of involving other key players in mediation sessions and offers some guiding principles and advice on managing the process.

Traditionally, particularly in family mediation, the meetings are between the two key players; in the case of family mediation, this is the parents. In other dispute contexts such as community and commercial, there may be significant others who need to be included. In community mediation in particular, practitioners may be involved in 'multiparty' meetings including representatives, for example, of police, housing departments, residents' associations, race relations, social work, probation, etc. Self-evidently, such events call for substantial management control over the process and possibly the involvement of several skilled mediators. A key question in determining who should be involved is: To what extent do the key parties involved in the dispute have the power to agree and implement any decisions made for a settlement? If the key parties don't have this power, then who does? Who might have the power to sabotage any agreement unless they are made 'part of the solution'?

Some key principles

- There needs be a clear justification for bringing other people into the process.

- The other person(s) (OP) should be identified as having a potentially significant and positive part to play in meetings that is likely to empower the key disputants (KDs) to negotiate effectively.

- It seems clear that whilst not being one of the KDs in the dispute, the OP has a significant role and/or vested interest in the case dynamics.

- The particular role the OP will play in meetings must be clearly defined, understood and likely to be adhered to.
- All parties must be in agreement with the involvement of the OP in part or for all of the process.
- Before the start of the full joint session, each KD and their elected OP should be seen together to recap on any ground rules and confirm their commitment.
- Positions in the mediation room should reflect the primary rights and responsibilities of the KDs. Generally this means that they sit 'centre stage', with their elected OP near but at a greater distance from them.
- The session should start with a brief recap on roles and a reminder of any ground rules agreed.
- It is common for some heated exchanges between any of the parties to occur, and this must be managed with respect through summaries of positions expressed and reminders of principles and objectives agreed. Ideally, this can be done in full session, but if not, use of caucus or a period of shuttle may be required so as to re-focus and lower conflict levels.
- It may be beneficial to have a brief review with the KDs just near the end of the session so as to ensure that they were satisfied with the process and outcome. Again, this symbolises their primary responsibilities and monitors any concerns about possible intimidation by OPs. The case referred to in Chapter 4 – of the young Muslim woman involved in a workplace dispute – is an example of the significant benefits of auditing the outcome with KDs. In certain traditional cultures, women may expect to be represented by a family member, rather than speak for themselves. This may not have been a problem in that particular case, but it is useful to check that she feels satisfied with the outcome, for herself as well as the family.

How the above principles translate in practice

Self-evidently, setting up meetings to include OPs will take longer, which will obviously have extra resource implications. It may be that the initial request for the involvement of an OP will come from one of the KDs at their mediation information and assessment meeting. The reasons behind their request can be explored in detail and, if seen to be constructive and beneficial to the outcome, will need to be explored with the other KD when seen at their MIAM. If they have already been seen, it may be acceptable to contact them by phone to explore their reaction and view. They may express some specific expectations about the proposal, for example wanting to set some particular ground rules. They may also request the involvement of an OP to accompany them, which will, of course, mean exploring that with the other KD. If the possible involvement of an OP does not arise at the MIAM, it may emerge as a possible option during the meeting with the KDs.

CASE STUDY: The need for a new partner to be included in a mediation meeting

Di and Ian were trying mediation in an attempt to resolve conflict over contact arrangements for their children, Sally (six) and Tom (eight). They had been divorced for some six months after Ian had moved in with Sara, a work colleague. Regular staying contact had been agreed but Di had stopped this and was offering visiting contact in the former marital home, which she said could be 'frequent' and unplanned. At the solo MIAM, Di claimed that Ian and Sara were spending substantial amounts on expensive gifts and treats for the children, despite Ian frequently being behind with child support payments. She saw this as seriously disadvantaging her with the children since she was far less able to afford such treats from her income. Her view was that he was wanting to be the 'treats dad', possibly in an effort to assuage his guilt at leaving them. Allegedly, too, Ian would spend more time with Tom, taking him to watch sports such as football matches, and this often upset Sally. The children also complained that Ian would often spend time driving them around his various building site projects to check on progress. He seemed to think that this was all a part of contact time with them, but it meant that they were left in the car for long periods, which bored them. The children were usually allowed to stay up very late, which resulted in them being very tired and irritable when returned after a weekend. Their homework was usually returned uncompleted, increasing the responsibility on Di to help them catch up.

Finally, Di objected to the children being encouraged to call Sara 'Mum'. On exploring the idea of the 'treats dad' and this last concern, Di admitted to a fear that the children would eventually want to spend more time with their dad, and that Sara wanted to usurp her role as the children's 'real mum'.

Anecdotal evidence suggests that often the issues for a potential mediation agenda are presented in inverse proportion to their significance. For Di, all her points deserved attention, and she deserved respect for her order of presentation. However, she freely admits to a deep sense of betrayal by Ian and ongoing sadness at the loss of what she had believed had been a loving and close-knit relationship. Another hypothesis here is that the offer of frequent contact in the former family home may be rooted in a conscious or subconscious attempt to persuade a former partner to return to the family. A reciprocal strong objection to this contact offer from Sara might well be driven by similar concerns. Often after the initial 'honeymoon period', the complexities of negotiating and developing a new partnership may result in a period of challenging tensions for Ian and Sara. This in turn can sometimes manifest itself in increased efforts by the new spouse to scapegoat and define the birth mother as the problem parent in contact disputes.

For his part at the MIAM, Ian described feeling 'caught in the middle' of his ex-wife and his new partner and as if he were in a no-win tug-of-war battle. He expressed constant feelings of guilt over the effects of the divorce on Di and the children. He was clear that, for him, the marriage was at an end even before meeting Sara; hence, she was, in reality, the 'trigger' of this dispute, not the cause of his leaving. He described how the stress of the contact dispute alongside his business responsibilities was having a major negative impact on his mental health. As a result of the MIAMs, a joint meeting was set up for Ian and Di, which followed typical early patterns of high emotion and conflict. Di expressed mostly anger and blame towards Ian and Sara as the causes of the contact problems. Ian expressed mainly regret and guilt for his part in the issues, whilst steadfastly defending Sara from having any responsibility for the problems. Over the course of two meetings, various interim options were negotiated and seemed to be agreeable to Ian. These were focused on demands from Di and based on each of her grounds for stopping staying contact. Essentially, they defined her ground rules governing any future contact. She made it clear that contact would not be resumed unless she received written confirmation of the contact from Ian and Sara.

As often happens in such cases, Di emphasised that the 'new deal' had nothing to do with her personal position but was instead entirely rooted in a mother's concern for the best interests of her children. This is a relatively common assertion of ex-partners in their attempts to distance themselves from any personal issues. Not altogether surprisingly, the new deal requirements were totally rejected by Sara. She refuted Di's assertions, stating that she would not be dictated to by Di as to how she and Ian would behave with the children when they were in their care. She further threatened that unless the contact was reinstated, she would encourage Ian to take legal advice and initiate court proceedings to seek a contact order. The situation had quickly reached an impasse and seemed intractable.

It was at this point that the mediators, whilst emphasising their impartiality, respectfully intervened to explore what options Di and Ian had in addition to possible costly and stressful court proceedings. Having skilfully summarised each of Di and Ian's positions, such a conversation would typically involve something along the lines of the following:

> What seems clear is that both of you are trying your very best together to do what is best for the children. Despite that, it is also clear that there are still problems in negotiating acceptable

options. What is also clear is that there are now three significant adults in the lives and ongoing care of the children. Since your efforts together here have not so far brought about any significant progress, right now it all feels quite stuck. So this is perhaps a good time for you both, with our help, to consider where you go from here. If that feels appropriate for you both, one of the options you might like to consider is bringing Sara into a session. Whatever you are feeling about her, Di, we do know from long experience that the role of a step-parent is a difficult one. For example, how do they determine the boundaries of their role with the children? What, if any, sanctions can they apply to the children when Dad is not around? You as Mum will have things that you would like to say to her about these matters, and it might be more helpful if you and she could discuss them together face to face rather than via Ian. You may need time to mull that over, and if you are in any doubt, it will, of course, be your and Ian's decision. Of course we would be here to help manage those discussions constructively and in the best interests of Sally and Tom.

Unsurprisingly, such an intervention may stir up a strong negative emotional reaction from Di, in which case she and Ian can be encouraged to consider other options. Any such options tend to benefit from listing on a flip-chart and each explored in a cost-benefit analysis for all concerned. If that does not progress well, a further intervention strategy is to ask each parent what their worst fears would be if they are unable to negotiate an agreement in mediation.

This has been referred to by Fisher and Ury (1981) as their BATNA and WATNA. In other words, what would be their 'best alternative to a negotiated agreement' and what would be their 'worst alternative to a negotiated agreement'?

Once again, this is all about timing. In the case study above, the three-way sessions were set up, starting with a brief meeting with Di and Ian to confirm their commitment and update the mediator since the last session. This was followed by a similar brief meeting with Ian and Sara so as to confirm the commitment and clarify principles of constructive communications. The joint session began with individual historical positions and, predictably, some heated exchanges between Di and Sara. Skilfully and impartially summarised by the mediator, it was possible to move through the stages of option development and finally to an interim plan for renewed staying contact. Ian acknowledged the problems around indulging the children and the need to spend more time with Sally, to stop the building sites visits during contact days and to ensure an earlier bedtime the night before the return day. Sara, to her credit, convincingly spoke of no wish to usurp Di's place as the mother and readily agreed to the children calling her Sara. Both Ian and Sara demonstrated significant empathy towards Di on all the key issues. All three made a commitment to returning to mediation should there be any difficulties with implementing the plans.

This case, along with others in the chapter, usefully illustrate the complex mixture of substantive/practical and emotive issues. The former are frequently presented in the initial stages as the main issues. However, they are often in inverse order to the main issues and underpinned and driven by emotion. In such cases, any attempt to deal only with the substantive agenda items may well be likely to be sabotaged by the emotive. Mediators must be constantly alert to verbal and non-verbal clues regarding emotional matters and be prepared to facilitate their exploration. This is not to suggest that all referrals inevitably include underlying emotive factors. They may well be very straightforward substantive disputes, such as finance, contact, property, etc. In reality, the substantive issues are the most straightforward for reaching a settlement or 'cutting a deal'. Emotive agenda issues come second place in terms of their chance of agreement, but only if any such potential process inhibitors are surfaced and dealt with. Typical evidence of such underlying 'blockers' are when interim plans break down and impasse occurs.

Other examples from practice

In one particular socially deprived community characterised by low income and high unemployment, a significantly high percentage of referrals for family mediation involved very young single parents. Typically they had a very young baby, often the result of one or two sexual encounters, and often the parents had never lived together. Mediation was particularly difficult compared to couples who were separating after longer periods of relationship and shared housing. One key difference was that there was no scope for 'leveraging' on questions about how they had managed such conflicts together in the past. By comparison, longer-lasting relationships had commonly involved both parents taking an active part in all aspects of the care of the children. The young parents' referrals commonly centred on the father wanting regular unsupervised contact, including having the child stay over at his accommodation. Often, the mother would be objecting to unsupervised contact on the grounds that the father had no experience of managing the physical care. Contact disputes are often complex and can involve high levels of conflict and emotion and include allegations about parental competence. Here, however, with such young parents, there is a reality regarding the practical care of a child of sometimes between a few months to one or two years of age.

High conflict between these young parents was making supervised contact at the mother's house unrealistic. An analysis of referral numbers showed that this category accounted for as many as 30 per cent or more of cases. As a consultant to one such service, I facilitated team meetings to reflect on what could be done with the issues presented. Outcomes from such referrals showed poor results compared to work with cases of long-standing relationships. It seemed that by comparison with this latter category, there was a significant lack of spousal and parental experience in mediation to begin to move through the process towards a settlement. As a result, the father would either withdraw from seeking contact or escalate the dispute to a court application for a contact order. Sadly, either option could result in the child losing contact with their father. In an article titled 'One in Five Dads Lose Contact with Children when Families Break Up, Says Survey' one recent study reported as follows:

> According to new research it's been estimated that of Britain's 130,000 absent dads, one in five fathers lose contact with children from earlier relationships with more than one in five who live with second families never meeting the children born during earlier relationships. The research reveals that in total 129,000 fathers don't have any contact with their children and 300,000 do not pay any money to support them. The study carried out by NatCen research group and was based on a series of large-scale state and independent studies, including the British Household Panel Survey, which has followed the lives of more than 5,000 families for two decades. (DJS Research 2013)

If my hypothesis regarding the lack of parental experience was correct, the next question might be: Who in the daily lives of these young parents has any level of influence or authority? Who might these young parents still be inclined to go to for help or advice when in trouble or doubt as to what to do? The most likely answer would be their own parent(s) and/or older extended family members. In many cases, each young parent was still living at home with parents. Taking a line of enquiry with the young parents early in mediation would include exploring their respective grandparental relationships. Sadly, all too often grandparents had also become embroiled in the dispute and, in support of their child, taken sides and engaged in conflict with the others. In some cases, however, sets of grandparents may have managed to stay on good terms together and were equally troubled by the dispute between the young parents.

One key dynamic affecting the process had to do with the relationship between the child's maternal grandparents and the birth father. Where this was constructive both ways, the odds of a positive outcome were significantly enhanced. The same dynamic applied to the ongoing relationship between both sets of grandparents. Where neither of these 'ideals' were present, successful outcomes were still achievable, although tougher on the practitioners and needing clear, firm management. Given all of the above possibilities, the next move was how to get the referent influence and decision-making support into the room and mediation process. More will be said later as to how to set up and manage this arrangement, but implementing this line of enquiry in the service had a significantly constructive impact on agreement levels. This concept was never formally researched in the service, so hopefully readers may be minded to test it more rigorously.

CASE STUDY: Maternal grandmother attending a mediation meeting

At a family mediation information and assessment meeting, a mother of a two-year-old boy, Liz, asked if her mother, Jean, could be present in the session. Problems with the previous contact arrangements involved the child's special dietary needs and involvement of the father's, Gary's, new girlfriend in the child's care. Liz explained that she was still in the early stages of recovery from major gynaecological surgery and was still very shaky, physically and emotionally. She felt that Jean being present in the room would give her a sense of emotional support. With clarification that Jean would have no active involvement in negotiations, Gary supported the plan and added that he still had very positive feelings about Jean. The session went well and new contact plans were negotiated, including an agreement for a return to mediation if there were any problems in implementation. Jean was positioned well back and out of sight of the parents so as to symbolise their primary status in negotiation. Just as the session was being concluded, Liz turned to her mum and asked if that all sounded OK to her. In a moving moment, Jean congratulated them both on the way they had dealt with the process. She touchingly said to Liz that deep down she knew that Gary could be relied on to do everything to ensure that their son was safe and protected. No subsequent requests for further sessions were requested.

CASE STUDY: Two new partners of divorced parents joining the mediation meeting

The parents of a young boy, Jake, aged 12, had divorced and for some three years had successfully operated a three-weekly alternating joint parental care arrangement. The child's school was conveniently located equidistant between the parents' houses, and the routine had worked well. Problems started when the mother, Sarah, started a relationship with a man, Charles, who lived about 100 miles away. She announced her plan to move in with Charles and to take Jake with her, offering a regular contact plan for the father, Paul. Paul was furious and quickly made an application to the court for a parental care order for Jake. A number of court appearances, including reports from a Children and Family Court Advisory and Support Service (Cafcass) officer and child consultant, failed to achieve a settlement, as did a series of mediation sessions.

The parents decided to escalate the case to the high court, declaring that since they could not resolve the matter, it should be the responsibility of a high court judge to rule what was best for Jake. A mediation process was set up with the sole objective of negotiating a detailed plan for how Jake was to be told of the court judgement and moved the same day to whichever parent won the case. Both parents made it clear that no attempt should be made by the mediators to negotiate on matters of residence or contact. They also wished that Charles also attend and contribute to the session. Details would be given later as to the protocol for setting up such a joint session, but it seemed clear that it should go ahead. The meeting called on the co-workers to exercise very active management control of the session. Coincidentally, both Paul and Charles were senior university lecturers in the same subject. The consequence was that both were highly articulate and tended to want to take control of the debate. The agreed seating plan put the parents 'centre stage' and with Charles some distance to one side of Sarah. Nevertheless, both men demonstrated stereotypically 'alpha male' personalities and academic language debating styles. This largely excluded Sarah, who appeared to be quite prepared to let the two of them battle it out. The skilled and experienced mediators had to frequently remind them of agreed negotiated ground rules and signalled the possible need for a time-out caucus, or ending the meeting altogether. They also managed to regularly re-focus the attention of the adults on what was best for Jake. An agreement was subsequently achieved on what and how Jake would be told the outcome decision together with an outline plan for contact with the non-resident parent. Disputes where one parent moves a long distance from the home of the other, including moves to another country, are not uncommon and are often highly charged. Where a new contact plan is achieved, it often results in an equal amount of contact time being spent by children with each parent over the year, but simply to a very different formula than before.

CASE STUDY: Maternal and paternal grandparents meeting together with a mother to resolve a child contact dispute

This case involved a joint mediation session involving Tanya, mother of a three-year-old girl, Abi, and both sets of grandparents. Before the birth, the father, Zak, had left the area, resisted efforts to arrange contact and, by moving frequently, had avoided efforts to enforce child support contributions. The focus of the dispute was that the paternal grandparents (PGPs) were aggrieved that they had never been allowed unsupervised contact and had very little involvement with the day-to-day life of Abi. Both sets of grandparents were recently retired, and whilst not wealthy, were relatively secure financially. At her MIAM, Tanya described her frustration and sadness at being trapped in the high level of conflict between the grandparents and extended family members. The conflict had escalated when the PGPs threatened to apply for a court order for regular contact. By agreement, a joint meeting was arranged with agreed protocol and ground rules involving both sets of grandparents and Tanya.

In this instance, the key disputants were the grandparents, but with Tanya clearly linked to what in her opinion was best for Abi. Conflict and emotions were high from the start, with PGPs claiming that they had been deliberately excluded from a fair share of involvement in the life of Abi. The main driver for this, they believed, was that they were being scapegoated for the behaviour of their admittedly 'irresponsible' son. The maternal grandparents' (MGPs') position was that the so-called 'feckless' Zak and his parents had consistently failed to help with child support. As a consequence, the full financial and lifestyle burden had fallen on them; therefore, the PGPs did not deserve involvement.

Skilled co-workers respectfully summarised and demonstrated impartiality and respect for each person's current position. Having achieved that credibility they were able to remind all of the reality that they were all in the room together because of their love for Abi. This intervention, like so many, is all about timing. Attempts to explore options for change before participants experience being heard and understood are unlikely to be effective. Known as 'mutualising', it also draws attention to what they all have in common. Before that intervention, disputants often start from an assumption that there is no common ground between them. That having worked, the mediators enabled a proposed move to a 'needs-led' discussion on how each side would like things to change, and what they would be prepared to offer. As often happens, this stage of negotiation also highlighted additional benefits for all sides. Greater involvement for the PGPs in the daily life of Abi would not only bring more free time for the MGPs in their retirement but also more financial support. Both outcomes were an obvious relief for Tanya and would facilitate her plans to train as a nurse. From that point, it was relatively easy to move to the final stage of drafting an agreement on the contact details.

CASE STUDY: Each client's independent legal advisor joining a mediation session

This example was brought to a PPC session and involved an Asian couple in the process of divorce. The issues for mediation included the children's residence, contact arrangements, finance and property matters. Conflict was at a relatively low level, but both parents were totally unwilling to confirm any negotiated options until they had each sought advice from their independent legal advisors. Not only was this protracting the usual mediation time span but also involved significant additional costs. Seeking advice and opinions is usually recommended by mediators.

However, anecdotal experience showed that timing played a key part in this legal advice seeking step. As well as the cost factor, if too early in the mediation process, conflict may be at its highest and trust at its lowest. As a consequence, it was not unusual that each party returned to mediation with distorted and rigid bids strongly in their favour. Commonly each legal advisor would have given an opinion on a percentage scale of typical settlement options. The parties would often table only the upper figure from that scale, adding that their lawyer had advised settling for nothing less. During the first mediation session, whilst encouraging the appointment of a legal advisor for each, mediators would add that the couple may find it wise to wait until the option development stage before seeking advice. By that time, hopefully, the conflict and trust balance will have been inverted. Financial assets and liabilities will have been verified and documented and hopefully a number of potential options listed. Increasingly, parties would also request the lawyers' opinions and advice to be documented so as to ensure transparency in the next mediation session.

To return to this case, the mediators were asked if they knew both legal advisors, and whether they were known to be non-adversarial. Both lawyers were well known to the service and encouraging of mediation for clients. Generally speaking, legal advisors do not attend mediation sessions, but my proposal was that, subject to agreement with the clients, the lawyers should be invited to attend the next session. Each client was seen in caucus with their lawyer so as to clarify roles and ground rules on if, when and how the lawyers would be involved. The transformation was remarkable, with each party clearly reassured by the presence of their advisor sitting near but at a distance from the key players. Often it took only a nod from their advisors to affirm the wisdom and safety of the main options and proposals in that one meeting. Subject to the draft outcome agreement being completed by mediators, a date was agreed for one last session to check and affirm the proposed settlement.

The Greek chorus and family ghosts

As a variation on the above section, it is worth considering what impact and influence others may be having on the capacity of disputants to negotiate a settlement. The term 'Greek chorus' derives from early Greek theatre productions that would use a group on one side of the stage to give a live-running commentary and insights for the audience on the unfolding drama. In mediation, it is often used to describe significant others connected with the main disputants, for example extended family members and friends, who typically take sides and stand by one party against the other. It is relatively rare for family or friends to refuse to do this and stay connected to both disputants. As the dispute progresses into a full-blown conflict, each clients' supporters tend to 'fan the flames' and help each party to embroider their idiosyncratic narrative of the history of the dispute. Commonly, their contributions include recommendations as to how to discredit and disempower the other side.

Mediators must be aware that, whilst they may be sitting in a room working with just two people, metaphorically standing behind each client there is often a substantial partisan group. In cases of high conflict and emotion, practitioners may need to include exploring the extent to which others are, or are not, supportive of their search for a settlement. Such a search can also be initiated if and when the parties put together detailed plans and a potential agreement. Whilst congratulating the clients on their work together, useful mediator questions might be along the lines of 'Who else in your family and friendship networks is likely to be happy and supportive of your plans?' and 'Who else might be less supportive, and would it help you both to explain your plans to them, and consider now how you will deal with their concerns?' Anecdotally I have found this anticipatory resistance discourse with non-Western communitarian cultures especially helpful. In such cultures, extended family and community pressures can be of significant influence and power on the parties.

To move on to 'family ghosts', practitioners need to be alert to past histories of each parent regarding any significant experience of their parents' separation. This is not to suggest that enquiring into such personal details should be standard practice with all couples coming for help. It should instead be one of a series of intervention options where emotional 'drivers' may be at the root of ongoing conflict and possible impasse.

CASE STUDY: Family ghosts

Steve and Kay were attending mediation to resolve issues regarding contact arrangements for their two children, Tanya (seven) and Sam (eight). In mediation, both presented as a low conflict couple with a pervading sense of sadness at the ending of their marriage. It took four sessions to reach an agreement, and in the last few minutes of each one Kay would become very tearful. Each time, she declined to say what was making her so upset until asked again at the final meeting. She explained that her parents had divorced when she was seven, the same age as Tanya. From that point on, every contact time each parent 'grilled' her for detailed information about the other and made her carry angry letters to and from them. She had found that so very upsetting it had left her wishing she did not have to continue the contact arrangement. As the tears flowed, she said that here she was now an adult, married with two children, and yet her parents were still doing it to her to this day.

At this point, she pointed at Steve and said that he too had 'history'. Steve explained that his parents had also divorced when he was seven and, allegedly on the grounds of his mother's objection to contact, he never saw his father again. After he had married Kay, she encouraged him to try to find his dad. It took over a year until, with the help of the Salvation Army, he found and was reunited with his dad. His dad was thrilled to be back in contact and to spend time with his grandchildren. One year later he died of cancer.

The reader might like to consider for a moment what, if anything, they might have said to Kay and Steve at that moment, in the silence that followed. As the mediator, and not for the first or last time, I struggled to think of what to say. My contemplation was not an issue since my sense was that the silence was 'reflective' and entirely appropriate. (For more on silence, see Whatling 2012, pp.71–74). Eventually, I said something along the lines of 'I find it hard to think of what to say right now. What does occur to me though is that you two know better than any expert in the world about what each of your kids need from you both, now and in the future. That means you can use that experience and understanding to decide together how to do it wisely and well, or to do what your parents did. Knowing you as I do now, and how much you care about and love them, I am confident that you will make the right decisions about that.' As often, I ended by saying that should they have any problems implementing the plans, they knew where I was and what and how I did what I did, so they could always come back. The tears stopped. Kay hugged me and Steve shook my hand warmly, saying 'Thanks, mate.'

Conjoint mediation and therapy (CoMeT)

A little-known development pioneered in Australia involves a model using co-workers, one a mediator, the other a family therapist. It was developed in response to a number of what had come to be known as 'high maintenance' couples. This term came from the fact that, whilst making up a relatively small percentage of divorcing couples, these couples nevertheless consumed substantial costs in courts' time and legal advice resources. It was as if, on the one hand, they were unable to stay together, yet found it impossible to divorce, and were constantly going back for court orders. Some years ago, on a study tour in Australia, I was able to explore this process with practitioners and researchers. Whilst controversial in terms of how we have traditionally defined mediation, early outcome results seemed to indicate that it deserves more research. The model is described as follows:

> In CoMeT sessions, relational issues that both clinicians and both parents agree what may be intruding on conflict

> management tasks are addressed 'up front' and by consent. If and when appropriate, the therapist, in consultation with the mediator, seeks the prior permission of the clients to 'open up' and explore personal meanings behind specific issues that appear to be impacting on settling the dispute. This 'opening up' is intended to assist in its own right. At the same time, the assistance is necessarily limited and primarily in the service of conflict reduction and conflict management. When this primary aim is reached, the therapist hands responsibility for continuing the process back to the mediator. The therapist remains in the room and continues to offer general support for the mediation process, just as the mediator remains in the room as a supportive witness to the therapeutic work. (Smyth and Maloney 2003, p.177)

What seemed to be crucial here was that the couple had a very clear understanding of what they were signing up for, so as to be able to make an informed choice to try it. This principle is helpfully highlighted by the researchers:

> When divorce mediation was in its infancy, definitions of what mediation was *not* were especially important. Mediation was *not* negotiation or litigation or therapy. At the same time, in her concerns about the potential to confuse mediation with therapy, Kelly was making an important plea for transparency that continues to have relevance. Knowledge and consent together remain an important cornerstone of ethical service delivery. (Smyth and Maloney 2003, p.164)

This statement underscores my own position on the potential for therapeutic models of mediation. In other words, it may be less to do with what is right or wrong than with exploring a bespoke model designed for every referral and avoiding one-size-fits-all and off-the-peg models. For a more detailed description of the model and research outcomes, see Smyth and Maloney (2003).

References

ACAS (2013) *Mediation: An Approach to Resolving Workplace Issues: A Guide*. Accessed on 16/09/2020 at https://archive.acas.org.uk/media/949/Mediation-An-approach-to-resolving-workplace-issues/pdf.

DJS Research (2013) *One in Five Dads Lose Contact with Children when Families Break Up, Says Survey*. Accessed on 16/09/2020 at https://www.djsresearch.co.uk/CentralGovernmentMarketResearchInsightsAndFindings/article/One-in-Five-Dads-Lose-Contact-With-Children-When-Families-Break-Up-Says-Survey-01428#:~:text=contact%40djsresearch.com-,One%20in%20Five%20Dads%20Lose%20Contact%20With,Families%20Break%20Up%2C%20Says%20Survey&text=The%20research%20found%20that%20fathers,after%20their%20family%20breaks%20up

Fisher, R. and Ury, W. (1981) *Getting to Yes: Negotiating Agreement Without Giving In*. London: Business Books Ltd.

Fisher, T. (1987) Towards a Model for Co-Working in Family Conciliation. *British Journal of Social Work 17*, 4, 365–382.

Parkinson, L. (1997) *Family Mediation*. London: Sweet & Maxwell.

Roberts, M. (2014) *Mediation in Family Disputes: Principles of Practice* (4th edition). Farnham: Ashgate Publishing.

Smyth, B. and Maloney, L. (2003) Therapeutic Divorce Mediation: Strengths, Limitations and Future Directions. *Journal of Family Studies 55*, 3, 404–416.

Whatling, T. (2012) *Mediation Skills and Strategies: A Practical Guide*. London: Jessica Kingsley Publishers.

CHAPTER 7

The Significance of Emotion and High Conflict in Dispute Resolution and the Management of Safe Practice

This chapter explores differences in the recognition of emotion and high conflict (EHC) across different dispute resolution contexts. It also considers the importance of screening for safe practice in mediation and offers a range of strategic questions for practitioners to use at the pre-mediation assessment stage.

'Different strokes for different folks'

This 20th-century proverb, meaning that everyone has their own way of doing things, usefully introduces the debate about how different mediation practitioners regard the usefulness or otherwise of emotion and high conflict in their work.

Anecdotal evidence from practice and consultation indicates that EHC is primarily associated with family mediation. This assumption tends to flow from the intensity of intimate spousal relationships compared to relationships in the workplace and the commercial sector. Typical organisational structures such as rank, titles and hierarchies can easily obscure the everyday underlying normal experience of emotional conflict. By contrast to family mediation, it may be that such different contexts reduce the risk of physical violence. Mediators also need to take account of significant differences in status between disputants that may result in conscious or subconscious intimidation and pressure to settle.

Some cultural implications

Cultural and sub-cultural differences also play a major part in the extent to which expression of conflict is acceptable. In his excellent text on 'embodied conflict', Hicks refers to how:

> The meaning of a given perceptual stimulus may vary by culture. For example, all humans ravenously monitor faces, along with bodily movement generally, for information about safety and danger, approval and dismissal, agreement and disagreement, acceptance and rejection… A diverted gaze will appear within one culture as a sign of deceit or lack of attention but will be a sign of respect in another culture. An intent direct gaze will be experienced as an insult or sign of aggression in one culture and as an indication of honesty, openness to relationship, or attentive engagement in another. (Hicks 2018, p.67)

Culture may also be powerfully influenced by matters of shame, honour and face-saving. Whilst these issues may be of some concern in Western individualist cultures, they are often of far greater influence in non-Western communitarian communities. For example, let us consider the ideas of 'lien' and 'mien' in Chinese culture.

> *Lien* is the respect of the group for a man with a good moral reputation: the man who will fulfill his obligations regardless of the hardships involved, who under all circumstances shows himself a decent human being. It represents the confidence of society in the integrity of ego's moral character, the loss of which makes it impossible to function properly within the community. *Lien* is both a social sanction for enforcing moral standards and an internalized sanction. (Chin Hu 1944, p.45)

Mien-tzd, stands for the kind of prestige that is emphasized in this country: a reputation achieved through getting on in life, through success and ostentation. (Chin Hu 1944, p.45–46)

The loss of such social and personal status and the resulting shame commonly makes life for the individual unbearable, often leading to suicide. From substantial personal training, experience over ten years of direct involvement with communitarian cultures shows how 'face' shame and honour are matters of major personal and social importance. In turn, they reflect the public status, not just for the individual and extended family and wider faith community. I have also had experience of training mediators who had a high number of referrals from the Chinese community. Mediating with first-, second- and third-generation family members required substantial cultural awareness, sensitivity, respect and competence if all members of a family were to agree to meet together, let alone negotiate family reconciliation. For more detail of these cultural issues and importance to mediation, see Chapter 3, 'Difference Matters'.

Practice implications of difference

How can we account for such differences and what implications are there for practice?

To explore this question of differences in EHC further, it is interesting to note that dispute contexts other than family mediation make little if any reference to these issues. The reasons for this difference merits further exploration. The nearest example to family mediation in a 'social relationships' context is probably community mediation. Disputes between neighbours may be potentially more liable to reach a level where EHC leads to acts of violence. Greater recognition of this risk was facilitated when the College of Mediators (formerly the UK College of Family Mediators) expanded its membership to include all mediation practitioners in any context. As a consequence, this independent regulatory organisation sets standards for the practice and supervisory requirements of its members. It also assesses training providers and their curriculum content and process as part of their approval process. For example, for COM practitioner members:

> 4.8 Safe Participation in the Process
>
> 4.8.1 For mediation to be effective all participants should feel safe to be involved in the process and to freely communicate their interests and concerns without fear of punishment or repercussion. Fear of harm may indicate domestic abuse within personal relationships, or bullying or harassment within workplace, neighbourhood and other settings. In all cases mediators must seek to discover through a separate screening procedure with each participant whether there is fear of abuse or any other harm and whether it is alleged that any participant has been or is likely to be abusive towards another. Where abuse is alleged or suspected, mediators must discuss whether any participant wishes to take part in mediation and consider with them where they might access other support services.
>
> 4.8.2 Where mediation does take place, consideration must be given to any practical arrangements that can be put in place to ensure the comfort and safety of all involved. (College of Mediators 2017)

Notice in particular the specific reference to 'workplace, neighbourhood and other settings'. Extensive online searches have failed to identify any mediation or training provider, or regulatory body, other than family and community mediation that refers to these issues and standards. However, the COM training provider registration and curriculum standards require:

> Mediator self awareness and development – Responses to own and observed conflict – Prejudice awareness and reduction – Self management in volatile situations. (College of Mediators 2013, Appendix B)

How has it come about that, apart from family and community

providers, there is this disconnection in the recognition of EHC? It seems somewhat akin to a collective professional avoidance culture – an 'elephant in the room'. Significant experience of working as a PPC with a major UK union with over a million members has left no doubt in my mind that the mediators were struggling with a substantial workload of staff disputes. Primarily centred on disciplinary and grievance procedures, they were mostly described as involving very high levels of EHC for all parties regardless of status, which in turn created serious difficulties for understaffed HR teams and in-house mediators.

What form do such human emotions take?

In dispute resolution, normal human emotional reactions such as anger, fear, hurt and, most toxic of all, frustration are all very near the surface. As a result, when threat and conflict is close, we react in a 'fight or flight' response. Biologically, this response is commonly described as an autonomic response, to a signal without the immediate intervention of the brain. It is also known as a 'lower-brain' reaction – the reaction is triggered by the spinal column. This is akin to pulling a hand off a hot surface. It needs no 'higher-brain' analysis of what actions to take. Such analysis commonly occurs after the initial response, and will often result in learning and memory that over time will recognise such threats as the hot plate and avoid repetition. It is highly probable that even at the highest level of major international corporation disputes, such as breach of contract or intellectual property rights, individuals will be experiencing everyday gut-level emotional reactions. Indeed, in world politics the same dynamics apply, often with very serious threats to world peace and stability. The past year or so has witnessed certain individual world leaders showing scant regard for traditional diplomatic language and protocol in publicly aired international communications, including the increasing uncensored use of social media.

Skilled and experienced mediation practitioners learn how

to read the signs of escalating emotion and its constructive management. By this strategic process, they create conditions for calm reflective discourse. Even slowing down the pace of speech and a calm, relaxed, open posture facilitates an inner 'higher-brain' analysis for clients. This internal discourse tends to result in a more rational assessment of the risks to self and others if self-control is lost. In turn, this usually moves on to memory scanning and recall of similar past experiences of self and/or others about the socio-legal sanctions for violence to others. Practitioners also need to understand how the lower-brain response triggers chemicals that fuel the physical responses to threat. Adrenaline is produced to reinforce the capacity to stay and fight, whereas the strength to run away is facilitated by noradrenaline. Little is known about why some people produce more of one than the other, but it may be a combination of genetics, gender and social conditioning. The key issue for mediation and high conflict management is that in the case of a 'flight fuel high', it may take up to one hour for the effects to wear off. For more detail on issues of safe practice and examples of questions that can be asked, see Chapters 5 and 7 in Whatling (2012).

Emotion and high conflict practice implications

To return to the earlier references to difference, the key issues incorporate two levels of analysis and subsequent questions. First, to what extent is EHC a factor across the whole range of dispute resolution? Second, if it is a common factor, to what extent is it acknowledged, surfaced, facilitated and managed by practitioners? From experience and peer consultation discussions over many years, I am in no doubt whatsoever that EHC is normal, axiomatic and universal in all dispute resolution contexts. Early extensive online searches, other than in family and community mediation, revealed no references to theory, research, training or codes of practice on this topic. Enquiries on these issues over recent weeks with two major UK providers of civil and commercial mediation practice and training have thus far not been responded to. Deeper levels of search and key words finally resulted in a US article that covered all the key issues underpinning my hypothesis, including research, theory and potential practice implications. At the time of writing I have also had the good fortune to be alerted by a colleague to a UK writer who also provides a valuable contribution to this largely neglected debate. The authors of the US paper introduce their study by stating:

> Although the recent literature on negotiation and mediation indicates the important role of emotion in the conflict process, few guidelines have been developed to assist new mediators in addressing parties' emotions during the mediation session. This study starts with the premise that attention to parties' underlying emotional experience is pivotal to achieving conflict transformation. (Jameson et al. 2010, p.25)

> Previous scholars have pointed out the centrality of emotion in conflict, suggesting that conflict transformation requires attention to emotion (Galtung 1996; Jones 2005). (Jameson et al. 2010, p.26)

These comments usefully endorse my hypothesis on EHC and the two key questions referred to above. Note too the reference to 'conflict transformation' as opposed to more conventional outcome objectives such as 'future-focused problem-solving', 'agreement' or 'settlement'. The clear implication here is that there may be a longer-term benefit to people involved in a dispute if EHC is transformed rather than just resolved. It has long been thought that one of the serendipitous benefits of mediation is that the parties may have learned from the process and be better able to resolve personal disputes in future. It is not unreasonable to assume also that going through a conflict transformation experience may have a similar added benefit bonus. Consequently, mediators who employ emotion-focused strategies may be more likely to bring underlying issues to the surface, increase understanding, and facilitate conflict transformation. Having provided detailed theoretical accounts of the meaning of emotion, the writers add:

> Because of the cognitive aspect of emotion, we believe that through facilitated discussion, parties can contemplate their own and the other's emotional experience, lending clarity to the conflict issues and their importance, and helping the parties identify possible areas of common ground... Improved ability to communicate our emotional experience should improve self-efficacy and allow all parties to feel more in control of the process. (Jameson et al. 2010, p.27)

This last sentence usefully reinforces a key principle of 'facilitative and transformative mediation' models, namely that of client empowerment and process control. Other studies referred to by the authors include references to the training of mediators:

> Schreier's (2002) research on emotional intelligence and mediation training indicates that the field of mediation suffers from a lack of attention to emotion and its consequences. She found that 'close to half of the respondents [mediators], including two-thirds of those with the most experience, thought that mediation training does not sufficiently teach how to address the parties' emotional reactions' (Schreier 2002: 107). (Jameson et al. 2010, p.31)

With the reality of resource limitations and cost factors, with so much to cram into foundation training programmes, it is unlikely that much can be done to remedy this shortfall. However, it should be highlighted as appropriate for continuing professional development (CPD) courses. Anecdotally, recent peer requests for CPD workshops support this training need, and it is driven by significant increases in high conflict at intake and assessment stages. In their post-research analysis discussion, the authors return to this training issue:

> Our assumption is that this is a necessary first step in developing and implementing an emotion-focused training component for new and experienced mediators. We identified five emotion-eliciting strategies used by mediators in a role-play scenario and suggest that these strategies – grant legitimacy, encourage emotion identification, confront avoidance of emotion, paraphrase emotion, and encourage emotional perspective taking, have practical implications for mediation training… We noted that some of the most interesting outcomes of these strategies occurred when they were used in concert. (Jameson et al. 2010, p.40)

There is a comparison here with my own previous work referring to 'concatenation' – on how the effectiveness of key strategic interventions, such as summarising, paraphrasing, mutualising and reframing, can generate a 'total greater than the sum of its parts' effect when delivered 'in concert' (Whatling 2012, p.133).

In their conclusions, Jameson et al. (2010) also refer usefully to the previously mentioned concept of 'face'. Under the heading 'Implications for Practice' they add:

> One of the difficulties new mediators face is knowing which questions will lead disputants to identify and discuss their underlying concerns and interests. This is particularly difficult when disputants seek to 'save face' and make a good impression with other organizational members with whom they are in conflict. (Jameson et al. 2010, p.45)

The authors conclude with six specific key recommendations for improvement of training curricula.

Throughout the evolutionary development of mediation practice, especially in North America and the UK, opinions have been divided on the question of how far past history and emotion should be facilitated. For more of the history and practitioner positions on this issue see Chapter 8, 'Mediating High Conflict Matters'. The case for its facilitation is persuasively made by one writer as:

> We make the distinction between what we call 'emotional' and 'rational' responses only because our complex brain allows for what we call thinking, characterised by logic and reason. There is also a tradition that claims that emotion and reason are in opposition and that to maintain control and to be able to make sound decisions, emotions should be minimised and rationally maximised. (Churchland 2002, p.219 in Hicks 2018, p.158)

However, another writer challenges this position:

> Selective reduction of emotion is at least as prejudicial for rationality as excessive emotion. It certainly does not seem true that reason stands to gain from operating without the leverage of emotion. On the contrary, emotion probably assists reasoning, especially when it comes to personal and social matters, involving risk and conflict. It is obvious that emotional upheavals can lead to irrational decisions. The neurological evidence simply suggests that the selective absence of emotion is a problem. Well-targeted and well-deployed emotion seems to be a support system without which the evidence of reason cannot operate properly. (Damasio 1999, pp.41–42 in Hicks 2018, p.132)

The above opinions add substantial support to practitioners who value the surfacing and facilitation of emotion and develop the capacity to empower clients to use its energy for the constructive process of change.

CASE STUDY: A training case example

Some months ago I was asked to provide a CPD workshop on high conflict to a family mediation team. The team manager was having difficulty in convincing the team of the importance of facilitating emotion rather than attempting to suppress or control it. This was particularly problematic when co-working with a team colleague since they were often lacking in strategic intervention mutuality and congruence. Apart from the manager and one other mediator, the team of seven were all from lawyer mediator backgrounds. They had all trained with the same training providers, all of whom were also from a legal background, as were their own practice consultants. Within the first few minutes, as part of the usual round of introductions, it emerged that they had all been told categorically by their trainers, on the subject of high emotion and conflict, to 'stay well away from it', 'do not go there' and to 'nip it in the bud before it gets out of hand'.

It is interesting to note how the professional background and orientations of mediation trainers reflect the mores and traditions of those they were trained by. With experience, they then become practice consultants and hence these adopted practice principles and styles are passed on. Fortunately, the team in this example were well motivated and open to exploring the issues and, by the end of the workshop, were genuinely committed to developing their constructive management of EHC. Post-training follow-up showed that all had made significant progress and were keen to do more in-house training on this topic.

To return to the second source of reference on these issues in Damasio's (1999) work, an author working primarily in civil and commercial practice states:

> All conflict involves people, and so all conflict is inevitably 'personal'. Without people, there would be no conflict, and people are never without emotions. So emotions are ever-present. (Randolph 2016, p.43)

> We need to understand how they inform our behaviour; how best to manage them when they present themselves in parties in mediation; and how to channel them for the constructive benefit of conflict resolution (Randolph 2016, p.44). Such emotions may need to be accepted by the mediator in a non-judgemental manner, so that they may be absorbed, defused and possibly deflected (Randolph 2016, p.45). The revelatory nature of emotions is habitually overlooked or underestimated by mediators. The display of emotions is likely to reveal the roots

of the dispute: what it is that triggered such anger; what it was that caused such hurt, grief, sorrow, disappointment, alienation or loss of trust. These are the realities of the conflict so why should the mediator shield the parties from this reality? It is neither required nor is it helpful to protect parties from the emotions that form the very essence of and underpin the entirety of the conflict. (Randolph 2016, p.48)

This selection of early statements leaves no doubt as to the author's position in the longstanding debate about the relevance of EHC in mediation practice. The ideas affirm the importance of the practitioner to adopt a demonstrative attitude of non-judgementality, professional curiosity, a non-patronising respect for disputants' ability to share the key emotions and an overall recognition of the normality of emotion. They are unusual in the sense that the author worked primarily in the field of civil and commercial mediation as well as practising as a barrister: professions not usually associated with the facilitation of emotion. It seems highly likely that his longstanding involvement in psychotherapy practice and teaching, alongside his other specialist activities, accounts for his capacity for synthesising the issues in such a convincing style.

He highlights such dispute resolution professionals' ambivalence further when he states:

The unpredictability of people's behaviour under high emotions evokes an anxiety in us because we are unsure how to deal with it. The principal concern of all those present – the mediator, the parties, their legal advisors and any others in attendance – is likely to be directed at the uncertainty and unpredictability of the outcome. 'This is getting out of control; where will it all lead?' The mediator, however, can profit from taking the time to explore and investigate such displays of emotion when they are presented. (Randolph 2016, p.49)

Here again the writer demonstrates his clear position on the effects that clients' emotion impacts on different professionals and settings in dispute resolution pathways. It reaffirms the reality that it is not a question of whether or not EHC exists but instead how it is managed constructively. It should be noted too that emotion facilitative practitioners are not immune from a degree of natural anxiety about the extent to which it is 'getting out of control' and 'where it will all lead'. The difference is that such practitioners are trained to understand their own and others' experiences of EHC, how to manage it at a constructive level and its benefits as a source of 'change energy'. Trainees frequently want to know how, where and when to intervene in EHC exchanges. Before moving prematurely to 'shut it down', experienced mediators learn to listen to and observe its 'quality'. Does it look and sound relatively even-handed? Did each party seem to be generally 'giving as good as they were getting'? Did it look and sound normal and cathartic, in terms of people needing to 'get it off their chests'?

Assuming that indicators of fight/flight reactions and hormonal production were not evident, then if the answers to such questions is affirmative, then let it be. It actually takes quite a lot of energy to maintain a EHC discourse, and when left to take its course it tends to run out of steam quite soon. For more detail on what to say and do when it cools down or escalates, and other EHC management strategies, see Whatling (2012).

Another key point raised by Randolph is the question of invasiveness and depth of such explorative digging. As a former family therapist and trainer for some 20 years, I spent much of that time considering the same question together with associated issues related to exploring past history. My view then and now as a mediator was that the depth and duration of 'excavating' should be in proportion to achieving 'good enough' knowledge and understanding to be able to work forwards with clients on the changes they needed to make for the future. It should not be invasive past the point of the 'good enough' test that was calculated professionally. If the balance of past understanding was subsequently found to be inadequate, some further digging would become self-evident and should be appropriately proportionate. This professional stance highlights significant differences between traditional long-term psychoanalytic models and more recent short-term and time-limited interventions in psychotherapy. Finally, despite his championing of EHC facilitation, Randolph reminds us of the need for practitioners to take responsibility for its constructive management. He comments on how historically, as far back as Aristotle, a 'master and slave' image of conflict evolved. Reason was seen as the 'master' of emotion, whereas emotion was the 'slave'. He adds:

> In conflict, the reverse is invariably true, emotion is the master and reason the slave. Reason fails to control emotion: indeed, passion seems wholly to overwhelm logic. The greater the stakes and the more critical the outcome, the greater the emotion and the more scant the rational logic. When parties are in dispute their ability to think rationally seems to diminish, if not completely disappear. The description of experiences such as 'the red mist descending' or 'I'm so angry I cannot think straight' are not uncommon. It may also be characterised by a sudden loss of temper, or behaviour described as 'out of character' or even more extreme 'losing it'. We often give advice to others to 'sleep on it' in order to feel differently the following day – and we do indeed have a differing perspective in the cold light of a new day. (Randolph 2016, p.53)

Here the author reminds us of another strategy, the benefit of calling for a 'time-out' to calm down. Where this usefully links is to my earlier references to face saving. Proposing a break for tea or a solo caucus or agreeing an interim arrangement and setting a date to review the plan are all useful strategies. When apparently at an impasse, it is surprising how different disputants behave when they return after a break. The break gives them the opportunity to reflect on their own behaviour and part in the impasse. This is often then reflected in their new positional statements by such comments as 'I have decided that for the sake of restoring our former relationship and all concerned I am willing to agree the following…' In saying this they are ostensibly bidding for a moral high-ground position, but also finding a way to protect their 'face'.

First, do no harm

To return to the earlier references to screening for safe practice, 'first, do no harm' is the principle that requires humanitarian actors to endeavour not to cause further damage and suffering as a result of their actions. Most commonly associated with medicine and the Hippocratic Oath sworn by doctors, the above quote is useful since it includes 'humanitarian actors', and hence mediation practitioners. It also provides a useful professional benchmark, since in our enthusiasm for the benefits of mediation, we must ensure that we do not overlook essential risk assessments.

The use of questions in screening and safe practice in mediation

Picking up on the training case study above, and returning to the initial safe practice focus, it seems appropriate to look again at questions about questions. Questions are the bread and butter of strategic mediation practice, especially when of the non-leading, open-ended type. Ideally, they are used purposefully and with strategic intent, rather than just randomly plucked out of the air.

Some examples of impartial non-leading, open-ended questions:

- What do you imagine it would feel like if you were to come to a joint mediation meeting with a person and/or people involved in the dispute?

- How easy or hard might it be for you to take a full part in mediation?

- What, if anything, might make it difficult to speak about what you want and need from mediation, and what would help you with that?

- How would you describe any arguments between you during recent weeks or months leading up to the referral to mediation?

- How similar or different has that been to how it was between you before?

- If the relationship between you changed significantly, how long ago was that and what happened to cause that?

- When you disagree, what does it sound like or look like, and how does it usually end up?

- When you have an argument, does the same person always win, or might it go either way?

- What happens if someone gets so heated that people find it hard to control their temper? What effect does that have?

- What sort of things might trigger such high conflict during an argument?

- When things get heated has anything been damaged or broken?

- What was the worst ever ending to such an argument?

Circular questions

Circular questions require a person to put themselves in the other's shoes and think about how the other may be feeling. Some examples of circular questions:

- What might the other person say about the extent to which they feel inhibited by you?

- What might they say about the extent to which they think you feel inhibited by them?

- How comfortable do you think the other person might feel about sitting in the same mediation room as you?

- How worried or concerned might they be about things you say or do in a joint meeting?

- Who might they say always wins or loses when there are disagreements?

Contextually framed questions

The idea behind this style of questioning is that some people may be unsure as to why they are being asked such questions or where the mediator is coming from. Such questions may also be more sensitive to individual differences in cognitive thinking styles. Evidence of any such uncertainty, confusion or resistance is often indicated by evasive responses and/or non-verbal signs of discomfort. The following examples are designed to signal purpose and intent:

- We know that it can be hard for some people to come to somewhere like this and feel confident that they will be free to say what they need or want to say. How far might that be a problem for you?

- Sometimes people have reasons to worry about what will happen if they speak honestly and openly about what has been happening and what they want from mediation. How far would you say that might be a problem for you?

The lists are not all-inclusive and can be added to as practitioners learn from regular reflective practice as to which questions are more or less useful in the screening process.

Screening for safety and facilitation of emotion

This chapter has aimed to draw together two different but potentially interconnected strands related to mediation practice.

The two different strands of screening for safety and facilitation of emotion are not usually addressed together in mediation literature. Indeed, the latter has been traditionally discouraged by writers and trainers on the grounds that it may trigger loss of control and potential violence. It has also highlighted the significant traditional differences in the extent to which emotion is explored in dispute resolution contexts. As mentioned in the text, the issues are contentious, and opinions often polarised between practitioners as to the importance and relevance of past history and emotion. Nothing in the discourse should be taken as in any way detracting from practitioners' primary responsibility for the safety of clients and themselves. Skilled practitioners constantly scan and monitor the quality of constructive expressed emotion and conflict temperature levels every second and should be capable of intervening to ensure safety of all involved. Equally, the debate should not be taken as suggesting that expressed emotion and high conflict are present in all disputes or need inclusion in the resolution process. Disputes do not of themselves have to escalate into conflict and are effectively resolved without recourse to mediation. Ultimately, it will be important for the reader to consider these issues and, having read the text, to decide where they stand and the extent to which, if at all, it changes their perspective or practice.

References

Chin Hu, H. (1944) The Chinese Concepts of 'Face'. *American Anthropologist* 46, 1, 45–64.

Churchland, P.S. (2002) *Brain-Wise: Studies in Neurophilosophy*. Cambridge, MA: Bradford Books.

College of Mediators (2013) Training Provider Registration and Curriculum Standards. College of Mediators.

College of Mediators (2017) Code of Practice for Mediators. College of Mediators.

Damasio, A. (1999) *The Feeling of What Happens: Body and Emotion in the Making of Consciousness*. New York: Pantheon Books.

Hicks, T. (2018) *Embodied Conflict: The Neural Basis of Conflict and Communication*. New York: Routledge.

Jameson, J.K., Bodtker, A.M. and Linker, T. (2010) Facilitating Conflict Transformation: Mediator Strategies for Eliciting Emotional Communication in a Workplace. *Harvard Negotiation Journal 26*, 1, 25–48.

Randolph, P. (2016) *The Psychology of Conflict: Mediating in an Adverse World*. London: Bloomsbury.

Schreier, L.S. (2002) Emotional Intelligence and Mediation Training. *Conflict Resolution Quarterly 20*, 99–119.

Whatling, T. (2012) *Mediation Skills and Strategies: A Practical Guide*. London: Jessica Kingsley Publishers.

CHAPTER 8

Mediating High Conflict Matters

This edited chapter was originally published as an article in The Journal of Mediation and Applied Conflict Analysis, *the National University of Ireland, Maynooth, 2017, volume 4, issue 1 and reproduced with consent of the editor and publication.*

To what extent is practice and training adapting to meet the challenge of an increase in high conflict levels in dispute resolution, including developments in social media and electronic communications?

This chapter explores the extent to which patterns of conflict behaviour by clients in mediation has been changing over time, and how far ADR practitioners and training are adapting to such changes. It provides some theoretical frameworks related to conflict behaviour and conflict ideologies that can be applied to practice. It also revisits some traditional conflict management styles, assumptions and values, and questions the extent to which these may benefit from evolutionary adaptation. It explores recent developments in electronic and social mass media communications and the impact these have had on conflict behaviour. It considers the extent to which recent conflict behaviours may need to be challenged more overtly through a more pro-active mentoring dialogue. Finally, it concludes with some recommendations as to how such challenges and ideas for change can co-exist with the principles associated with facilitative mediation.

Exploring some changes

Anecdotal evidence from mediation practitioners indicates that the conflict behaviour of mediation clients has changed significantly over the past few years. Increasingly, disputants come with learned styles of conflict resolution significantly different to those previously encountered by mediation practitioners.

Shifts in client conflict behaviour may increasingly challenge some traditional mediation principles. Being mindful of these essential principles in practice is to believe that, by definition, clients should be regarded as the experts in their circumstances and subjective universe. This being so, they are also, by definition, the experts in their own conflict and dispute situation. It follows that they are best placed to resolve the problem(s), not least because they will have to take personal responsibility for implementing any changes, actions and agreements made in mediation.

Donald Schön is also helpful when he writes:

> What is the kind of knowing in which competent practitioners engage? How is professional knowing like and unlike the kinds of knowledge presented in academic textbooks, scientific papers and learned journals? Indeed practitioners themselves often reveal a capacity for reflection on their intuitive knowing in the midst of action and sometimes use this capacity to cope with the unique, uncertain and conflicted situations of practice. (Schön 1983, pp.viii–ix)

My sense is that Schön is identifying significant differences between formal academic learning, study and reading compared with the everyday learning that practitioners gather from their clients. This style of learning – what Schön calls 'knowing in practice' – is frequently at a semi-conscious or unconscious/intuitive level. Such knowing can be accessed and articulated through discussion and supervisory consultation based on exploratory questioning, at which point it rises to a conscious level. My own anecdotal experience ranged from work as a university academic lecturer, and later as a National Vocational

Qualifications (NVQ) assessor of professional practitioners. That experience brought me many rich examples of the differences in their learning styles and their ability to articulate their knowledge. Neither was of itself greater or lesser in practice outcome terms, just different.

Over the decades of development in mediation, a recurring debate relates to the extent to which it should include dealing with emotion. One writer describes emotions as:

> Both a cause and escalator of conflict, and positive feeling among the parties are often a key component of resolution. Once one accepts that emotion is the foundation of all conflict, the issue of how emotion influences the management of conflict becomes central. Many theorists have begun to point out that the lack of detailed attention paid to emotions and their role in relationships limits our understanding of conflict and that more work needs to be done to remedy this. ... Often trying to suppress or dampen the emotions may simply lead to resentment and the breakdown of agreements. Parties may try to disrupt the process because they do not feel heard, or refuse to follow through with an agreement because their feelings were not recognized. ... Feelings that may dissuade parties from agreeing to a negotiated settlement that appears in all other respects to be reasonable include distrust, anger, fear, contempt, embarrassment, shame, pride, and disappointment. As a result of negative feelings, one party may be antagonistic and resist anything the other party proposes. ... Helping parties to communicate and acknowledge their emotions is key to the restoration of healthy relationships. (Maiese 2005, p.1)

Conflict ideologies and life scripts

As referred to in Chapter 1, 'Transitions', we have all evolved personal 'life scripts' about conflict. We may have come to regard conflict as potentially exciting, creative, energising and positive. Alternatively, we may see it as worrying, potentially painful and essentially negative This notion of 'life scripts' is amplified by other writers:

> Our analysis of mediation – as a form of conflict discourse shaped by ideology – is grounded on two premises derived from recent studies of the construction and representation of ideology in everyday discourse. The first premise is that 'ideologies' are organising frameworks that people use to view, interpret, and judge their surrounding world. Although ideologies are often held as cognitive values or expectations, they are acquired and expressed through social phenomena; people learn (and recreate) ideologies through participation in groups and relationships (Billig et al. 1988). (Folger and Jones 1994, p.7)

As well as developing individual conflict ideologies, people are substantially influenced by absorbed cultural ideologies. Mediators also acquire professional conflict ideologies. This triadic influence needs to be understood if practitioners are to develop the essential capacity to both listen and think outside of their personal, cultural and professional conflict ideology boxes.

As discussed in Chapter 3, 'Difference Matters', some useful contemporary labels for this capacity are 'cultural intelligence', 'cultural competence' and 'cultural fluency'. To take the latter as a particularly helpful example:

> Cultural fluency arises from knowing something about the lenses that we look through and then learning from the surprises we encounter as we come to glimpse the world through others' lenses. In this way we begin to anticipate, internalise, express and navigate in unfamiliar systems. (LeBaron and Pillay 2006, p.187)

Gaining clients' co-operation by understanding their conflict styles

Ideally this work is done pre-mediation, with each client seen separately. During that time valuable information can be gathered from each disputant regarding their particular conflict patterns and ideology. Clients are likely to be aware of what upsets and angers them, and how they tend to react when that happens. For example, they may use such metaphors as 'When X happens, I usually kick off, blow a fuse, freak out, go ballistic…'

Open-ended questions can be used strategically so as to build up an understanding of how such metaphorical terms translate into actions and consequences. For example, a mediator might ask:

- What sorts of things happen to cause you to kick off?

- Can you give me an example of how you might be feeling inside when that happens?

- If it came to any similar upset or argument in mediation, how do you think you might react, and how might I recognise that it was happening to you?

Once such cause-and-effect consequences are more concretely identified, the discourse can progress on to questions about what might help the individual and other parties involved to maintain the conflict at a constructive level.

On the issue of pre-mediation work with each party separately, others have also referred to the benefits of the separate meeting:

> In our experience, it is in these separate meetings that a lot of the major work of the mediation is done. In these meetings, the mediator works carefully with each of the parties to construct a frame of meaning around the problem issue. We are thinking mainly of situations where there are entrenched disputes that make it difficult for the parties to talk freely in front of each other. (Winslade and Monk 2001, p.137)

From this model of separate meetings, each party has the benefit of uninterrupted space and time. The mediator is in turn able to give the speaker 'free attention' and active empathic listening, free also from any risk of the other party interpreting verbal or non-verbal mediator responses as possible evidence of partiality.

Neurolinguistics and personal constructs

The Oxford English Dictionary defines neurolinguistics as: 'The branch of linguistics dealing with the relationship between language and the structure and functioning of the brain.'

At its simplest, the study of neurolinguistics concerns itself with the idea that all humans develop personal perceptions of reality, or what can be termed 'mental constructs', that are in turn reflected in the particular words they use. Applying such concepts to mediation practice suggests that there may be benefits in listening very carefully to particular words used by clients so as to begin to comprehend their deeper meaning. Where the words relate to the more powerful emotions encapsulated in their stories, the mediator can usefully adopt the same words in their reflective responses. In doing so, the aim is to demonstrate a concern to stay true to the clients' internal frames of reference. As an example of this technique, in a community, workplace or family dispute, one party may refer to a stage when 'it all goes ballistic again', and the other may respond with 'Yes, and then you just lose the plot and end up walking away again'.

The mediator can adopt these frames of reference and use the same words, both in reflective summaries and when referring to the disputants' potential options for the future. So with the above example we might say: 'From what you are each saying, it sounds like it might be really helpful right now if you could all think about what you need, and what else could be done differently, so as to avoid things going ballistic, or anyone losing the plot and walking out. Perhaps at least for the next few weeks or months, because it sounds like it's hard to get anything sorted between you when that happens.' The idea is that the constructs embedded in the language used have important symbolic meaning for each individual.

Bear baiting and medieval barbarism revisited

For one contemporary example of sociological and generational changes in conflict behaviour, consider the potential modelling effect of the Jeremy Kyle show, which has been variously described as follows:

> Many people love The Jeremy Kyle Show. With a consistent audience of about 1.5 million it has been a staple of the ITV daytime schedule for almost a decade. Younger viewers, in particular, seem to find the presenter addictive. You can buy T-shirts with slogans such as 'Don't mess with Jezza'…
>
> One of the most damning critiques of Kyle's show was made by a Manchester judge, Alan Berg, in 2007 as he sentenced David Staniforth to a £300 fine for headbutting a fellow guest on the programme. 'It is for no more and no less than titillating members of the public who have nothing better to do with their mornings than sit and watch this show, which is a human form of bear-baiting which goes under the guise of entertainment.' (Burrell 2013)

Judge Berg was quoted as saying:

> It seems to me that the purpose of this show is to effect a morbid and depressing display of dysfunctional people whose lives are in turmoil, often in some perceived or actual dispute with each other for the purposes of titillating bored members of the public who have nothing better to do in the morning than watch trash TV.
>
> It is less a show than a form of human bear-baiting – that is how I see it – which goes under the guise of entertainment. It should not surprise anyone that these people, some of whom have limited intellects, become aggressive with each other. (Manchester Evening News 2007)

Such dispute resolution influences, together with the impact of contemporary technological communications such as email and texting, may well support the hypothesis underpinning this chapter – that there is value not only to trainee and novice practitioners, but also to experienced mediators who may, over time, have evolved their own style but without any particular training, common process or structural framework.

These technological communication advances may seem a relatively recent phenomenon. However, it is interesting to note that as far back as 1998, Deborah Tannen was writing about it, in a chapter entitled 'Fast Forward: Technologically Enhanced Aggression'. Under such sub-headings as 'E-Mail Aggravates Aggression' and 'One-Way Communication Breeds Contempt', she highlights such issues as:

> E-mail and now the internet and the World Wide Web, are creating networks of human connection unthinkable even a few years ago. But at the same time that technologically enhanced communication enable previously impossible loving contact, it also enhances hostile and distressing communication. As the ease of using the internet has resulted in more and more people logging on and sending messages to more and more others with whom they have a connection, it has also led to increased communication with strangers and this has resulted in 'flaming': vituperative messages that verbally attack. (Tannen 1998, pp.245–246)

Mediators practising in the workplace context have also noted a significant increase in disputes resulting from this technological communication revolution. Tannen also noted this over two decades ago:

> In my research on workplace communication, I found that a large percentage of serious conflicts had been sparked by one-way communication such as memos, voice mail, and e-mail. (Tannen 1998, p.248)

The author concludes the chapter with:

> The rising level of public aggression in our society seems directly

related to the increasing isolation in our lives... This isolation and the technology that enhances it is an ingredient in the argument culture. We seem to be better able at developing technological means of communication than at finding ways to temper the hostility that sometimes accompanies them. (Tannen 1998, p.262)

Tannen's key message here is that the development of widespread networks and enhanced technology has tended to result in more recipients being targeted, compared to previous communications by phone calls or letters. A consequence is that some recipients may not regard such messages as relevant or appropriate to them. The technology has also tended to encourage a more abrupt and abbreviated language style that lacks the quality of traditional communications. This more often rushed cryptic and style may well lead the recipient to feel offended and result in a retaliatory language and the beginning of a conflict spiral, especially when copied in to communication with other work colleagues, family members or friends.

The effect of narrative personal histories on conflict

Typically each of the parties in dispute has developed a personal idiosyncratic history of the minute details of the dispute. That historical record usually identifies itself as the victim, the trustworthy truth-sayer and the reasonable, rational party. Inevitably, the other party will be described as the antithesis of all those epithets. The longer the dispute has gone on, the more this history will have been embroidered and will include negative 'add-ons' so as to add weight to the alleged bad behaviour of the other party. This familiar story-weaving usually includes additional negative attributions regarding the other party, provided by the Greek chorus of family and friends.

Most mediators understand the importance of allowing these stories to be narrated, heard and understood in the initial assessment meeting and early stages of joint meetings. One writer usefully draws attention to this phenomenon:

> I would suggest that we need to re-think this storytelling process when it involves one or more parties with high conflict personalities... People with high-conflict personalities (HCPs) tend to be preoccupied with the past – defending their own behaviour (which is often a significant part of the problem)... Ironically, giving them an uninterrupted opportunity to tell their stories reinforces staying in the past and avoiding responsibility for the future – whether the story is about what happened yesterday, last month or years ago... some HCPs seem to get a 'high' from telling their stories, just as addicts get a 'high' from telling stories of their past experiences using drugs. (Eddy 2013, p.2)
>
> The stories also tend to place 100% of the responsibility on others – especially the other party or parties to the dispute... By the end of the story they hope that you will be persuaded:
>
> a. That they are totally not responsible for the problem or the solution.
>
> b. That the other party is totally the source of the problem.
>
> c. That you are the only one who can help them.
>
> The result of hearing this intense storytelling is that you, as the dispute resolver, feel stressed, angry and/or helpless, and eager to get the case over with to relieve your frustration. (Eddy 2013, p.3)

Assuming that the practitioner's initial intake assessment reveals this potential HCP in one or more parties, Eddy (2013, pp.1–6) goes on to give four particular suggestions for shifting the emphasis onto future problem-solving. Whilst the full text is in more detail and is recommended reading, they are summarised here as:

- 'Structure the process for problem-solving.' The parties should be helped to understand that the focus of mediation will be on problem-solving and the future, not on the past.

- 'Avoid getting emotionally hooked. Instead, respond with interest.' Impartiality can be maintained by summarising statements that focus on mutual empathy, attention and respect rather than individual points of view.

- 'Ask for proposals.' The future-focus principle can be demonstrated by regularly asking each person for their ideas and proposals for change, rather than what happened in the past. They may need help to frame such proposals in terms of what changes they *do want*, rather than what they *don't want*.

- 'Consider coaching before decision-making.' The single-party assessment process is the optimum stage for bonding and forming a trusting relationship with each party. The session can usefully end with teaching them how in the joint sessions their role is to contribute to future-focused problem-solving negotiations.

- 'HCPs always feel like victims (and many have been at one time), but we don't help them to allow them to hear their own stories over and over again.' Help the parties move on from historical perceptions of having been in the role of victim, which is relatively common for one or both, and is often a significant part of their story. Respectfully helping them to identify how to move forward can empower them with a sense of success and goals that they designed and can own.

That last sentence connects helpfully with the key issues expressed throughout this chapter.

So what?

As well as a good reflective question for mediators themselves as they formulate a potential hypothesis, this question can also be a valid question to put to the parties directly.

A typical example of such a question would be: 'So what are the implications of what just happened here in the room, or of what one party just said or did?' The question might usefully be extended to include: 'And in what way does what was said and done influence what we are all attempting to do here in mediation?'

How goes pre-mediation is how goes the mediation: Mentoring matters

Anyone can become angry – that is easy, but to be angry with the right person at the right time, and for the right purpose and in the right way – that is not within everyone's power and that is not easy.

Aristotle

Pre-mediation assessments in high conflict cases will inevitably raise questions and concerns regarding time and funding resources. However, it may well be that time spent on such activity will actually speed up and enhance the negotiation process, so may well not actually involve greater time or cost. It may also have a beneficial impact on conversion to mediation and/or reduce drop-out rates.

This approach may also involve difficult, challenging and straight-talking conversations about the practitioners' perceptions of clients' suitability for joint meetings.

Such conversations will only be effective if the practitioner has earned the respect of each client throughout the first meeting. This respect is earned through demonstrable, unconditional, positive regard; non-judgemental responsiveness; and empathic accurate listening together with validation of the client's perception of the history.

Assuming that this 'nettle grasping' phase of challenging conversations goes well, what are some of the options for mentoring? One option is to propose that all parties involved might consider committing to a set of 'constructive negotiation principles'.

Principles that help make mediation a constructive process

Mediation works best when all those involved in the meetings:

1. Take turns to speak and do not interrupt each other.

2. Call each other by first names, not 'he' or 'she' or indeed more pejorative labels.

3. Use 'I' statements – for example not 'he is always letting me down and hurting me' but 'I feel hurt and let down when _____ happens'.

4. Try to describe what they want, rather than what they don't want, i.e. what they would like other people *to do differently in future*, rather than what they *don't want them to do, or to stop doing*.

5. Try to avoid blaming or attacking others, or engaging in put-downs, and instead try to ask questions of each other for the purposes of clarifying and understanding them.

6. Try to avoid making rigid demands or taking fixed positions and instead express themselves in terms of their personal needs and interests and the outcomes that they wish to achieve.

7. Listen carefully when any one person is speaking to them and avoid interrupting.

8. Listen carefully and with an open mind with the intention of trying to understand the other person's needs and interests.

9. Recognise that, even if they do not agree with each other, each person is entitled to their own views and perspective.

10. Try to avoid dwelling on things that did not work in the past, or what people did wrongly, but instead try to focus on how they would like things to be done differently in the future.

11. Attempt to avoid unproductive arguing or expressing high emotion about the past history, and try instead to use the time in mediation to work towards the fairest and most constructive agreement possible.

12. Be able to speak up if they feel that something about the mediation process or meeting is not working for them.

13. Express their concerns if they feel the mediator is not being impartial or even-handed.

14. Feel able to ask to take a break when they need to.

15. Think about, and inform the mediator about, what, if any, more specific and personal principles that are not listed above that they may want added to the list.

These principles are aspirational and should be openly acknowledged as such with the parties, given that they do not in themselves offer a panacea to preventing the expression of natural emotions associated with disputes.

Clearly the content of this list of principles must be acceptable to all parties involved and should include scope for more potential bespoke and individual additions. Strategically they could be talked through in individual assessment meetings and clients encouraged to take them away, consider them in detail and come to a future meeting with any additional personal principles they might wish to add.

Social communication developments

Other recent electronic communication options, in particular texting, emails and Facebook, have increasingly featured in reports of conflict escalation across the range of ADR contexts.

Mediators engaging in a range of disputes could mentor disputants regarding the potential dangers of communicating about their dispute via these innovations.

As referred to above regarding a list of communication principles by disputants, so too might the use of email offer a similar list for adoption by mutual agreement.

Better to BIFF than bash

Continuing with this theme of adopting conflict reduction principles, such ideas can also apply to texting. As mentioned above, e-communications can be cryptic and, in the case of texts, are frequently abbreviated to letters rather than words, such as BTW in place of 'by the way'. Whilst this may be functional when time is limited, it can also lead to misunderstandings or rudeness. Verbal communications tend to package conversations in a language that makes it acceptable to the recipient but is commonly missing from a text.

One writer offers helpful advice on these issues that could be discussed in a mentoring role. The following are summary extracts and the full copy can be accessed:

> Do you need to respond? Much of hostile e-communication does not need a response. Letters from (ex-) spouses, angry neighbors, irritating co-workers, or attorneys do not usually have legal significance... Often, it is emotional venting aimed at relieving the writer's anxiety. If you respond with similar emotions and hostility, you will simply escalate things without satisfaction, and just get a new piece of hostile mail back. In most cases, you are better off not responding... If you need to respond, I recommend a BIFF Response®: Be **B**rief, **I**nformative, **F**riendly and **F**irm.
> (Eddy 2007)

Be brief. Going into too much detail can at times result in a spiral of conflicted two-way communication. In the words of the old saying 'least said soonest mended', be brief. The same principle applies to the respondent. Not rising to the bait will often delete it from future reference. Be informative and friendly. Keep responses friendly, brief, to the point and factually informative.

Avoid threats, or derogatory comments about the other person's behaviour, reputation or character. The longer you maintain the above principles and a respectfully assertive rather than aggressive manner, the harder it will be for the other person to respond negatively. Finally, be firm. In a non-threatening way, clearly outline and summarise for the other person your information or position on an issue.

Informed consent rules

In addressing some of these challenging issues, a recurring concern has been how to ensure that traditional ethical principles of facilitative mediation are safeguarded. Without such principles it risks being regarded as a licence for evaluative or directive mediation practice.

A number of key clarifying principles will hopefully discourage any such assumptions or inferences.

Using pre-mediation and mentoring meetings can address the nature of the 'deal' openly and frankly regarding how we will be working together in mediation.

When a mediator is considering a potentially challenging intervention about a participant's behaviour, it is likely to be more readily accepted if framed as an invitation. For example a mediator may say: 'Is it OK if I tell you what I have noticed about how you communicate together, and how I think that may be creating some potential problems in what you are trying to do here?' Whether or not the challenge is well received, it is likely that the invitation approach will reduce resistance.

Clients can also be invited to reject, disagree with or modify the challenge. Such challenges must be grounded in a relationship of mutual respect between practitioner and client that will have been earned from the earliest communication during the engaging stages of contact.

Challenging interventions must be rooted in a mediator hypothesis, based on objective, observed behaviour and communication patterns, not in some abstract and/or theoretical assumption. Such challenge should also ideally include ideas as to how any unhelpful communications can be improved on and/or reframed.

Challenges are often best preceded by questions as to how the parties feel the meeting is progressing, what I often refer to as 'process auditing'. Clients can also be invited to comment on how it feels emotionally when either of them communicates in a particular manner or style.

All of the above ideas must be firmly rooted in a facilitative mediation style and principles that relate to process issues, not the content or outcome agreement. The former is a legitimate conflict management responsibility of the practitioner. The detail of the latter belongs to the parties. The line between the two activities can be complex and easily confused, so mindfulness and a constant internal reflexive dialogue by practitioners is crucial.

References

Billig, M., Condor, S., Edwards, D., Gane, M., Middleton, D. and Radley, A. (1988) *Ideological Dilemmas: A Social Psychology of Everyday Thinking*. London: Sage.

Burrell, I. (2013, 5 April) *Jeremy Kyle: Judge, Jury and Exploiter?* The Independent. Accessed on 19/09/2020 at www.independent.co.uk/news/people/profiles/jeremy-kyle-judge-jury-and-exploiter-8562459.html

Eddy, B. (2007) *Responding to a Hostile Email*. Accessed on 19/09/2020 at www.highconflictinstitute.com/articles/mediation

Eddy, B. (2013) *When Storytelling Hurts Conflict Resolution: Some Tips for Dispute Resolvers*. Accessed on 12/01/2021 at www.highconflictinstitute.com/articles/mediation

Folger, J.P. and Jones, T.S. (1994) *New Directions in Mediation: Communication Research and Perspectives*. London: Sage.

LeBaron, G. and Pillay, V. (2006) *Conflict Across Cultures: A Unique Experience of Bridging Differences*. Boston, MA: Intercultural Press.

Maiese, M. (2005) 'Emotions.' In Burgess, G. and Burgess, H. (eds), *Beyond Intractability*. Conflict Information Consortium. University of Colorado, Boulder. Accessed on 28/01/21 at https://www.beyondintractability.org/essay/emotion

Manchester Evening News (2007, 25 September) *Jeremy Kyle Show Blasted*. Manchester Evening News. Accessed on 05/11/2020 at www.manchestereveningnews.co.uk/news/greater-manchester-news/jeremy-kyle-show-blasted-1005150

Schön, D. (1983) *The Reflective Practitioner: How Professionals Think in Action*. New York: Basic Books.
Swink, D. (2010) *Managing Conflicts with Email: Why It's So Tempting*. Accessed on 19/09/2020 at www.psychologytoday.com/gb/blog/threat-management/201001/managing-conflicts-email-why-its-so-tempting
Tannen, D. (1998) *The Argument Culture: Changing the Way We Argue*. London: Virago.
Winslade, J. and Monk, G. (2001) *Narrative Mediation: A New Approach to Conflict Resolution*. San Francisco: Jossey-Bass.

CHAPTER 9

Practising What We Preach Matters

To What Extent Do Mediators Apply the Expertise of Their Professional Craft to Managing Conflict in Their Daily Lives?

The cobbler's children have no shoes
The essence of this proverb describes the phenomenon whereby certain professionals are so busy with work for their customers that they neglect to use their skills to help those closest to them.

One writer usefully describes this as 'cobbler's children syndrome in the workplace':

> In many organizations I have encountered during my consulting career, people have complained about 'Cobbler's Children Syndrome'. Like the proverbial children of the shoemaker who go without shoes, I have consulted to technology companies that have outdated computer systems, marketing firms that don't market themselves in any way, and consulting firms that fail to put into practice for themself a single theory or model upon which they have built their businesses. Everyone who works in these organizations is aware of the irony of these situations, and yet it's very difficult for individuals, teams, or the organization as a whole to do anything to change the dynamic. Perhaps there is some deep psychological reason why the 'Cobbler's Children' dynamic exists… There may be a compensatory aspect to the

syndrome in that, for example, one suffers from some kind of weakness, and becomes acutely aware of it. Still struggling with it personally, you may know what it takes to help others deal with it. (Dattner 2008)

This chapter raises issues about the extent to which mediators, as experts in conflict resolution, are able to apply their bread-and-butter skills and strategies to conflicts that arise in their daily lives, with particular reference to conflict in the workplace and mediation organisations. In particular, it will:

- Name the 'elephant in the room' – to identify the problems that we all know exist to a greater or lesser degree – that in all organisations, conflict is inevitable, and just as common with mediation providers.
- Raise awareness as to the extent of the problem.
- Identify some common characteristics of the problem.
- Remind readers of the everyday professional methods of dispute resolution management.
- Offer some ideas for how such disputes might be managed.

For some three decades of active involvement with the development of mediation in the UK, I have witnessed conflicts between professional mediation colleagues that have been perplexing and at times seriously worrying.

The conflicts arising from these disputes have had all of the ingredients of potentially destructive conflict: the early idiosyncratic histories, the triggering event, the spark, the fanning of the flames and, in some instances, costly and distressing endings of partnerships. Such processes are all too familiar to mediators in their daily work with parties in dispute.

Over a period of a few weeks or months conflict narratives are written, line by line, into metaphorical chapters, that are to become the history books or so-called 'truths' of the facts and details. Sadly, as always, each person's history book relates substantially different accounts of what had led up to the rifts.

All too familiarly, sides are taken and friends duly stand by friends in support. The voices of the Greek chorus swell to help amplify and embroider the histories each time the latest chapter is narrated within the respective 'camps'.

As specialists in the field of dispute resolution know only too well, conflict in social and organisational environments is axiomatic. It is not a question of if conflict exists but how it is managed that matters. Without conflict, there would be very little. As one writer points out: 'Conflict can signal constructive ways of bringing about change and of re-ordering lives. At least the potential for positive change is greater when there is anger than where there is the helplessness and hopelessness of depression' (Roberts 2008, p.108).

People can become involved in many such constructive disputes without the process necessarily having to escalate into conflict. From anecdotal observation, such conflicts continue to occur in mediation organisations, despite the professionals' many years of developing understanding about how to manage them. They can have very serious consequences to individuals, the organisations concerned and potentially to bystanders within the wider professional orbit.

Such unprofessional behaviour might be less surprising if, for example, we compared this issue to other groups, such as accountants, lawyers, engineers, doctors or politicians. It might be hoped that they could manage disputes and conflicts wisely, but, by comparison with mediators, it would not be an issue so central to their core business and professional specialism. However, as mentioned above, when our mediation colleagues were in conflict, those of us practitioners connected were variously worried and frustrated by our colleagues' failure to apply their professional skills in resolving their own disputes. Commonly, such disputes often become 'dissolved' – for example by one side-stepping down or leaving – rather than 'resolved'. As a consequence, the unresolved feelings frequently get added to any future conflict in the organisation. For example, in major national organisations, such as coal mining, workers and their unions carried forward grievances from generations of families who had lost previous disputes. It was as though it was from a sense of duty to fathers and grandfathers before them to bring forward grievances that had little or nothing to do with the current conflict, as what are often referred to as 'add-ons'.

But it's different when it's us who are directly involved, isn't it?

We can understand what people mean when they say that, but no, it should not be different. Mediators open their doors to the public as experts in conflict management and dispute resolution, and should, therefore, be expected to manage it when it involves them personally.

In fact, it is all the more imperative that mediators 'practise what they preach' and 'put their money where their mouths are'. Not only must mediation and dispute resolution within the profession be done, it must be *seen* to be done.

Whilst my practice and training is primarily in family mediation, I have also delivered training in other contexts including community, health care complaints, victim-offender and workplace disputes, so I have had significant contact with their associated organisations. Over the past 20 years this also included delivering training programmes in some 15 different countries in East Asia, Africa, the Middle East, Europe and North America. From that experience, I can say that the issues covered in this chapter are by no means just a UK phenomenon. They are both universal and multi-cultural.

Arguably, experience in one mediation context may make it difficult for a practitioner to apply understanding and skills to a different context, such as their own workplace disputes. However, most conflict dynamics, processes, skills and strategies are universal across all contexts, so should be transferable, both in our comprehension and understanding.

So what then can be done? Some ideas for managing the conflicts

It is difficult to think of any potential new ideas to recommend for managing such disputes. So what follows is more of a reminder and a checklist of ideas, many of which will be very familiar to experienced mediators. It is equally difficult to offer advice and recommendations given how tied many mediators are to their standard forms of practice.

However, this may be a good point to remind readers of some of the core tenets of everyday practice in the business of dispute resolution. In other words, to the principles, values, knowledge, skills and strategies that mediators routinely deliver to their customers yet often seem unable to apply consistently when it involves them personally:

Search for the interests and needs that underpin positions.

Experienced mediators know well that magic moment when, through skilful and strategic use of questions, layers of shared interests, values and, more important still, shared fears and mutual needs are revealed. Many practitioners will recall the 'positions, interests and needs' (PIN) commonly used in training and referred to by Andrew Floyer Acland: 'Positions, interests and needs add up to a pyramid with often only the top third, the positions, actually visible when the mediation begins. It is so important to remember the other two-thirds, and the many ways in which they can remain hidden, that a further diagram is warranted: the PIN (positions Interests, needs) Pyramid' (Acland 1990, p.152).

The pyramid-shape Acland discusses is divided into three horizontal sections. Each section denotes a part of the PIN acronym. The top of the pyramid represents positions; the middle represents interests; the bottom represents needs. If we envisage this pyramid printed on a separate clear acetate sheet for each party laid side by side, there is no connection between their interests and needs. Through needs-led questions, the mediator starts to superimpose one sheet over the other, gradually drawing them closer together so that the common areas of interests and needs gradually overlap. The closer they are drawn together, the more two new sub-pyramids emerge as joint areas of common interests, and especially of joint needs.

For example, when company bosses and managers attempt to impose new contracts of employment terms and conditions without prior consultation with those who are directly affected by the changes, both sides tend to quickly assume polarised 'positions'. Typically these positions include positional statements by employers such as: 'Sign the new contracts now or face dismissal.' They may also add some moral pressure by citing the potentially serious financial consequences for the organisation unless the contracts are accepted. On the staff side the responses are commonly along the lines of: 'Impose those contracts and we will have no option but to withdraw our labour.' Before very long, such opening position statements tend to degenerate into even greater threats. As referred to above, the 'needs-led' analysis employed by mediators gradually moves people off their positions and uncovers underlying needs and fears of all sides, such as the need to maintain employment, jobs, income, productivity and customer services. In almost every case, there is also a need for a reduction in stress, distress and dis-ease. This frequently also involves a need to avoid the costs of resources that would be required in resorting to formal procedures such as tribunals, arbitration and litigation. It is commonplace to hear each party to the conflict speak of the other as being a 'control freak', 'refusing to step down or let go of control' and of 'adopting rigid positions' and threatening very serious actions unless the other side backs down.

Commonly, each side speaks of how they are 'only interested in the best interests of the organisation, productivity and customer services'. This style of communication relates to the 'positions' peak of the pyramid, and is usually referred to as 'positional bargaining'. Such bargaining is usually characterised by threats and counter threats about what each side will do, unless all their demands are met. The role of the mediator is to respectively acknowledge their positions yet invite each side to explore what their underlying wants, hopes and indeed needs are for a settlement. In the case of a workplace dispute, employers usually need an assurance of productivity and income so as to meet customer demands and avoid any risk of liquidation. On the workers side, they will usually be needing reliable jobs and wages to support their families. Once these underlying levels of the PIN wants and needs are 'on the table', the mediator can steer negotiations as to what would need to happen to ensure a 'win–win outcome' as opposed to a 'lose–lose'. Both sides tend to state that, try as they might, they simply cannot understand the other's issues, grievance or complaint and that it is the other side that refuses to engage in seeking a resolution.

Here I should own that despite knowing as much as I do about dispute resolution, I too am just as capable as any of us imperfect human beings of getting into interpersonal conflict. This occurs through a natural inclination, often by a fear of loss, towards adopting a rigid position, making threats and writing our own idiosyncratic narrative of the what, who and how of the dispute. Alas, if I were just half as good a person as I know how to be, I would be truly amazing.

What has changed over the years of involvement in dispute resolution is that after a few days or weeks, a little inner voice says something like: 'Hang on a minute, you know very well what is going on here and what you are doing by stoking the fire and fanning the flames. What this situation needs instead is for you to initiate a dialogue in which you ask the significant other(s) to talk about their wants, needs and concerns, and ask in return that they will listen to yours.' From such careful 'listening with understanding' activities will hopefully flow options and agreements as to how to resolve the dispute and re-establish good working relationships to the mutual benefit of all concerned.

Some recommendations

- Remember that alongside several attributes of a good mediator you must believe that the majority of people in dispute are capable of being (a) reasonable and (b) rational. The problem is that when they first come, they are often behaving in ways that are both very unreasonable and irrational.

- Remember to reframe the dispute and crisis as an opportunity for change and transformation, towards better understandings and the greater good, health and well-being of our institutions and professional colleagues.

- Despite how hard it is to resist at times, don't resort to the old 'personality clash' opt-out, a commonly used explanation by disputants to account for problems. In my early days of practice, I had a team colleague who from our many conversations and indeed arguments appeared to have nothing whatsoever in common with me. My main issue was her tendency to make disparaging and judgemental comments about some clients in team meetings. We both seemed to be aware that our values appeared to be so far at odds that we managed to avoid co-working together for a year or so. For my part, I was worried that these differences would impair our working partnership and become apparent to our clients. Eventually, it became clear that this avoidant behaviour was having a negative impact on the rest of the team. Discovering this, I invited her to discuss it, and as a result we agreed to work a case together. In reality, we worked very effectively together and continued to do so, with no demonstrable evidence of any of the conflicts of values I had feared.

In referring to this problem, one writer usefully discusses this issue: 'The only way I know of actually resolving a personality clash is head-on: by admitting the feeling and setting out to trace its causes. If this is done fully and honestly, looking at each other's:

- Values
- Opinions
- Assumptions about each other
- Prejudices about background, education, even accent or race then maybe the situation can be redeemed (Acland 1990, p.61).

- Use your primary communication organs proportionately – two ears, two eyes and one mouth. So do more listening and observing than speaking. Resist the temptation to interrupt with comments or disagreements until you have a good understanding of the other's issues. As Plato said, 'Wise men speak because they have something to say; fools because they have to say something.'

- Push for 'needs-led' discussions that identify not what you and the other(s) *don't* want, but what you all *do* want and need.

- Maintain 'adult-adult' transactions (Whatling 2001). Regardless of the number of 'crossed transactions' you get in response, the more you respond in 'adult-adult' problem-solving mode, the harder it is for the respondent to cross the transaction from 'controlling/critical parent' or 'rebellious/angry child'.

- Start from a life position of *I'm OK – You're OK* (Harris 1973 in Whatling 2012).

- Record and share the issues in a neutral mutual language.

- Never press the email or text 'send' button till you have slept on it, and recognise the damage that cryptic electronic communications can create in today's social, personal and professional world.

- Once the stories have been articulated and ventilated, push for future-focused SMART outcome objectives that are **S**pecific, **M**easurable, **A**chievable, **R**ealistic and **T**ime-bound. Such objectives should also be needs-led and include statements of principles against which to evaluate outcome agreements, for example a mutual commitment to early win/win settlements, and a return to former constructive and productive working relationships.

- Be 'hard on the problem and soft on the people'. Externalise the problem as an *it* rather than a *they*. This surprisingly powerful and effective technique had been described as 'externalising conversations' by Winslade and Monk. 'As mediators externalise a problem, they speak about it as if it were an external object or person exerting a negative influence on the parties but they do not identify it closely with one party or the other' (Winslade and Monk 2001, p.144).

    For example, a mediator would stop talking about the people who are causing the problem and instead would identify the issue that is responsible. It is not that the working partnership has broken down because a certain person 'fails to respond to emails' or 'is rude, manipulative or a bully'. Instead, it is a 'communication breakdown' or 'trust problem' that is what is preventing the resolution of the dispute – 'it' having come between the parties in dispute. The narrative-style mediator will often use an object such as a pen to symbolise the 'it', perhaps placing it down on the table between the disputants whilst talking about when and how it had come between them and caused such problems. Having thus externalised and objectified the problem, the mediator will invite the disputants to identify actions that might begin to remove the 'it' problem from the working relationship. This discourse will usually reinforce the symbolism by simultaneously removing the pen from between the parties. Like so many of the apparently simple techniques and strategies mediators use, it is surprising just how powerful this technique can be, particularly in the all-important business of face-saving.

- Resist the temptation to make threats at all costs. When we do that, it is usually a signal of desperation, and we are frequently not in a position to carry them through, with any less cost to us than the other side. As Haynes and Haynes (1989) put it: 'Threats are made out of weakness; promises are made out of strength' (p.42).

- Try to avoid the natural human temptation to engage in the psychological defence mechanism of 'displacement'. We are all bound to want to protect our own private (internal) and public (external) self-image or 'face'. When they hear a client say 'I know I wasn't always the ideal spouse/boss/business partner', the mediator knows only too well that the next word will be a resounding 'BUT', usually followed by a long list of the sins and failings of the other. To resist doing this is hard, since if we accept even 50 per cent of the blame or responsibility for what is going wrong, we will still find it hard to live with its negative impact on our self-image and self-esteem.

- 'Why beholdest thou the mote that is in thy brother's eye, but considerest not the beam that is in thine own eye?' (Matthew 7:3). This is also described as follows by Acland (1990, p.105): 'Conflict provides opportunities for people to express aspects of their personality which are normally kept hidden. More than this, people *project* on to others their own personality or behaviour: they accuse other people of doing things or behaving in ways in which they themselves are behaving, or want to behave.' What the writer is highlighting here is essentially a process of taking emotions or traits we dislike about ourselves and attributing them to someone else. An example might be of an unscrupulous business partner accusing a colleague of untrustworthy behaviour, to as to deflect attention away from themself. It has the effect of saving face and protecting our ego at times of stressful conflict.

- Ask for help from trusted colleagues who are known by both sides to be capable of being objective and impartial.

- Don't react or retaliate. A friend of mine going through divorce used to read me the latest inflammatory and goading letter from his wife's solicitor, followed by his own equally adversarial response. Many times I pointed out that by far the best way to end this war of words was to not react in a similar style. His response was inevitably that he just could not resist it. In effect he was enjoying the adrenaline rush and ritual of this 'game' despite the inevitable damaging side-effect it was having on his relationship with his children.

- Remember that win/win is not just the absence of win/lose or lose/lose, but an outcome where the total result of the outcome is greater than the sum of its parts. In other words, by engaging in constructive option development, we may well uncover hitherto unforeseen outcomes that are better for all concerned, including their organisations, than either side had previously identified.

But what if they won't play?

Mediator colleagues in dispute frequently tell of how, despite doing everything to engage the other side in dialogue, they just won't respond.

- Try some 'negotiation jujitsu', as so well defined by two writers as: 'If the other side announces a firm position, you may be tempted to criticise and reject it. If they criticise your proposal you may be tempted to defend it and dig yourself in. In short, if they push you hard, you will tend to push back. Yet if you do, you will end up playing the positional bargaining game. Rejecting their position only locks them in. And defending yourself sidetracks the negotiation into a clash of personalities. You will find yourself in a vicious cycle of attack and defence, and you will waste a lot of time and energy in useless pushing and pulling' (Fisher and Ury 1981, p.113).

    For more ideas on these issues see also *Getting Together* by Fisher and Brown (1989). Despite the dates of these texts, they remain as valid today as they were at publication. Mediators, professional practice consultants and trainers know well that clients, supervisees and trainees will frequently challenge their ideas and comments. A mature and confident practitioner will not be affronted by such challenges. Indeed they should welcome them as evidence that what they are saying conflicts to some degree with the personal constructs of the other person. Mediation is increasingly being recognised as more a craft than a science. It is indeed a social science rather than pure science. As a consequence, those who challenge our ideas may be just as right as us, or alternatively we may both be right, depending on different circumstances and life experiences. Consequently, 'negotiation jujitsu' would avoid the useless 'pushing and pulling' referred to above by Fisher and Ury.

We should resist the temptation to try to get our ideas pushed through by force of argument in an attempt to defeat the other. Instead, learning from martial arts techniques, we move to metaphorically stand beside the would-be opponent as though facing in the same direction. This tactical move diminishes head-to-head or eyeball-to-eyeball confrontation and resistance. The next move is to ask some simple questions such as: 'Given that we have some differing opinions on this, help me understand what some of the differences are from your experience. Then maybe we can talk about differences and similarities in our ideas and hopefully arrive at a better understanding in trying to move forward. I am really interested in your response to what I have said and would like to have more detail on what your concerns are about the differences, if that's OK with you? It sounds like it might help us to explore in a bit more detail any questions you have about what I have said in terms of how helpful or not my comments are and in terms of where we are trying to get to.' It is interesting to note that two of these examples include the journey metaphor. Conversely it is not uncommon to hear high conflict disputants use war metaphors such as destroying/obliterating/blowing out of the water to describe the arguments of the other side.

In conclusion, I often recall the wise words often spoken at training events by John Haynes, who described the mission of the mediator as searching for the good in people. To which he would usually add 'and you can choose whether you spell good with two o's or one'.

References

Acland, A.F. (1990) *A Sudden Outbreak of Common Sense: Managing Conflict Through Mediation*. London: Hutchinson.

Dattner, B. (2008) *Cobbler's Children Syndrome in the Workplace*. Psychology Today. Accessed on 20/09/2020 at www.psychologytoday.com/gb/blog/credit-and-blame-work/200812/cobblers-children-syndrome-in-the-workplace

Fisher, R. and Brown, S. (1989) *Getting Together: Building a Relationship that Gets to Yes*. London: Business Books Ltd.

Fisher, R. and Ury, W. (1981) *Getting to Yes: Negotiating Agreement Without Giving In*. London: Business Books Ltd.

Harris, T.A. (1973) *I'm OK – You're OK*. London: Pan.

Haynes, J. and Haynes, G. (1989) *Mediating Divorce: Casebook of Strategies for Successful Family Negotiations*. London: Jossey-Bass.

Roberts, M. (2008) *Mediation in Family Disputes: Principles of Practice* (3rd edition). Farnham: Ashgate Publishing.

Whatling, T. (2001) Transactional Analysis Matters: The Potential Application of Transactional Analysis to Mediation. *UK College of Family Mediation Journal 1*, 3, pp.1–6.

Whatling, T. (2012) *Mediation Skills and Strategies: A Practical Guide*. London: Jessica Kingsley Publishers.

Winslade, J. and Monk, G. (2001) *Narrative Mediation: A New Approach to Conflict Resolution*. San Francisco: Jossey-Bass.

CHAPTER 10

The Coronavirus Pandemic and Its Potential Effects on the Behaviour of People in Dispute

This chapter will explore a range of issues arising from the coronavirus pandemic, insofar as they potentially impact dispute resolution and mediation practice. It will define the crisis as a worldwide 'paradigm shift', raise questions regarding how behaviour will change in the face of the coronavirus pandemic and the extent to which it may have a positive or negative impact on dispute resolution. With particular regard to family mediation, it discusses a number of categories for typical dispute behaviour and how parents manage the process. It will also explore how different cultures manage disputes, the difference between individualist and communitarian cultures and how far the pandemic may influence such differences. Finally, it will explore how disputant conflict communications may change for good or bad, what the implications may be for practitioners and practitioners' intervention styles in facilitating constructive dialogues. It will also provide some case studies so as to illustrate parental communications on matters of residence and contact.

How things were developing one month into social isolation lockdown

At the time of writing, some four weeks into social isolation, there are reports of vexatious phone calls to the police reporting breaches of the social isolation protocol by another disputant in an attempt to invoke police investigations. Police chiefs were appealing to the public to stop such time-wasting calls. Similarly, there were already research reports of a sharp increase in cases of domestic abuse and deaths of abused mothers and children. Parliament was approving an urgent new domestic violence bill, including a substantial increase in finance for protection and support services.

The Guardian newspaper gave a lengthy editorial headed: 'UK lawyers inundated by divorced parents arguing over lockdown custody'. Specific examples included:

> Lawyers have been inundated with inquiries from divorced parents arguing about where their children should stay during the lockdown, with some trying to get their former partners sent to jail for breaking existing custody arrangements.
>
> Some parents have been using the coronavirus outbreak as an excuse to stop their ex from seeing the children, withholding access on spurious grounds including 'my ex won't be able to teach my child their times table'.
>
> One woman asked her lawyer to apply to a judge to send her ex to prison after he failed to pick up their child for a regular visit – despite him having proof he wouldn't have been able to get there 'for any amount of money'. Another wanted her husband to go to jail after he took the children to a different address from that stipulated on their court order in order to shield vulnerable relatives at the usual home. (Pidd 2020)

Some people were very opportunistic, trying to use the circumstances to cancel contact. While most clients have been able to agree alternative arrangements, sometimes using a mediator, around 20 per cent were using the crisis as a tool to stop contact or to hurt the other party, apparently without considering the potential impact on the long-term emotional well-being of their children. One obvious problem with such reports is that we have no data about those who are collaborating to do the best for their children, since they are less inclined to contact lawyers or mediators.

In terms of global impact, how do we categorise the pandemic?

The coronavirus pandemic probably qualifies for the label of a 'paradigm shift' (PS). Originally a strictly scientific term, it assumes that the usual and accepted way of doing or thinking about something changes completely and permanently. The idea of a paradigm shift has subsequently been accepted as applicable to the social sciences and applied sciences and hence to allow in its definition some lesser scientific changes. Examples now have been listed as the car production assembly line, document scanning, faxing and emailing. It might therefore not be unreasonable to apply PS to the coronavirus pandemic. In other words, despite our individual worldviews and perceptions of reality, it is as if everything we tended to assume we knew and understood to be axiomatic is suddenly and fundamentally changed. Life can never be the same again. For example, separation and divorce changes family life. For better or for worse, to not change is not an option for all family members, extended family and social and community networks.

The first key question to consider is how the experience of the coronavirus pandemic will change disputants' behaviour and their communications and how, in turn, that will change mediation practice. It seems likely that some such changes might be for the better, whilst others may be for the worst. For example, it may allow a transition from a spousal dispute, with their conflict-saturated dispute patterns, to a constructive parental focus. Practitioners are well used to facilitating that shift from positional arguments to needs-led negotiations, but for some, it may have historically taken more time than in a coronavirus pandemic world.

Some hypothetical categories of disputants' behaviour pre-coronavirus pandemic

What follows are anecdotal categories of how adults manage separation and divorce that may help in situating the analysis about the effects of the coronavirus pandemic. To the best of my knowledge, the categories have not been defined or published by others and have probably not been the subject of significant, if any, research. They will hopefully be regarded as generalisations rather than stereotypes. The key difference is that generalisations based on significant patterns of behaviour are adaptable to subsequent contradictory information and data. Stereotypes, on the other hand, tend to be maintained regardless of contradictory new data and are often linked to prejudicial actions.

1. Constructive parental separation (CPS)

2. Unconstructive parental separation (UPS)

3. Constructive with help from mediation and/or non-adversarial legal advisors (CWH)

4. Unconstructive involving legal action (ULA).

The categories in more detail:

1. **CPS.** A very interesting category that may be a particularly significant percentage of cases but one which is assumed to not generate useful research data. These parents may or may not have experienced conflict in early relationship breakdown, but they then arrive at a joint decision to part amicably and non-adversarially. Their choice may well be based on some or all of the following factors: a wish to retain the best elements of their previous relationship; concern for the best interests of any children; preservation

of extended family and friendship networks; important faith and/or cultural principles and imperatives; a wish to maximise assets and minimise legal costs.

One informative case example involved a couple who came to mediation requesting only an opinion on their draft proposals for a settlement, for subsequent more formal legally worded court documents. Another couple came for a series of mediation sessions on particularly complex financial settlement negotiations and with a history of high conflict. Given the conflict history, the negotiations in mediation were characterised by shared humour and some touching moments of caring concern for each other and the children. At the end of the process, this was referred to by the practitioner, noting how relatively unusual that was. It had also raised a question as to how far they were both still certain the marriage was at an end. After a long silence, the husband said that during the protracted high conflict stages, they had both psychologically and emotionally 'damaged' each other to the extent that there was no 'going back'. The wife agreed and added with great sadness that had they come to mediation at the start, the outcome could have been very different, and they may possibly have been able to reconcile.

2. **UPS.** Anecdotal evidence suggests that it is also a fairly common group, albeit yet again hard to quantify statistically, since they tend not to try mediation or legal advice. Their behaviour tends to be characterised by high open adversarial conflict, negative enmeshment of children, with partisan side-taking by extended family and friendship networks. Collateral damage is often substantial, with emotional scarring for the children in particular. Some anecdotal evidence comes from these children, when as adults they may come to mediation for their own separation and recount stories of how their parents had behaved. Interestingly, such couples often come

expressing a strong desire to avoid such negative outcomes for their own children.

3. **CWH.** An interesting cohort that is more familiar to mediation practitioners and family lawyers. They tend to be characterised by low open conflict patterns, high levels of mutual trust and non-adversarial child-centred values. Typically they seek professional help with negotiations on the grounds of wanting to be sure their plans are consistent with fairness and the parameters of court judgement criteria. Somewhat similar to the first category, they will often also be happy for each of their individual legal advisors to confer together in crafting a potential settlement for them. This beneficial, non-adversarial settlement route is often overlooked in debates about historical adversarial legal traditions. Such parents are also ideally suited more to facilitative, parental empowerment and transformative models of mediation than to settlement-seeking, directive, problem-solving styles.

4. **ULA.** Again, a more familiar cohort since they attract more publicity and present more challenging conflict behaviours to mediators, lawyers and the courts. They tend to present with high levels of open conflict in inverse proportion to low trust across all levels of evolved relationship principles, including former spousal, financial, parental and fidelity trust bonds. The idea here is that when forming a new spousal relationship, couples negotiate, or at least create certain mutual assumptions that will be the foundations of their relationship. A typical example of this phenomenon is where adultery – a breaking of the 'fidelity bond' – is so emotionally overwhelming for a partner that it results in an 'all bets are off' blanket rejection of all other bonds.

Experienced and skilled mediation practitioners are well used to facilitating a gradual transition that moves the discourse from a spousal dispute, to constructive restoration of the other's trust, in particular post-separation parenting plans. Sadly, for others, perhaps a minority, it involves a costly and time-consuming legal ritual of adversarial claims and counterclaims. Court judgements are often regarded as unsatisfactory by both sides, and there are commonly attempts to sabotage the orders, particularly on child contact and financial support. Quite often in such entrenched cases, a point is reached where lawyers and courts adopt a metaphorical 'washing of hands' and encourage a referral to mediation. Paradoxically this can sometimes result in a realisation by parents that the law in their experience has 'failed' to give them what they wished for, and so they settle down to a less adversarial discourse and settlement negotiations. Given the disputants' often high conflict history, such referrals can be very challenging, not least because the disputants have been 'trained' to channel their conflict behaviour into a court culture. This training involves coming to understand that their legal advisors need to be provided with a good continuous supply of pieces of evidence to present to the court for use against the other parent. It is essentially an 'evidence-led' culture and process. Early sessions in mediation must take account of this psychological acculturation, as clients typically continue to demonstrate this culture within their discourse. It may take between one and three sessions of 'retraining' to move towards a needs-led dialogue. An up-front open explanation with clients of this process difference is often essential.

One case involved a young couple who were so trapped in this evidence-led culture, developed over several months of court hearings, that they were incapable of making the switch. Over three sessions they were unable to have any conversation without recounting new specific events of poor parenting and child-risk behaviour by the other parent during court-ordered contact. The accounts were usually written down and often included offers from family and friends willing to act as witnesses. No amount of effort at challenging this evidence-led discourse had any effect whatsoever on either parent. They were repeatedly advised that if either was in any doubt about the ability of the other to safeguard the children, they should report their concerns to child protection services, since a mediation agreement could not offer child protection. Eventually, the couple were referred back to the probation-based Child and Family Court Advisory and Support Service (Cafcass). Fortunately, such actions are rare since the majority of parents understand the requirement to behave differently.

So what?

This wonderfully simple two-word question, much favoured by the late John Haynes, translates into mediation practice as 'So what are the implications of what we have just seen and heard from these clients in terms of the *what* and *how* of strategic practice?'

One of the earliest practical changes following the coronavirus pandemic and social distancing was a marked acceleration of online video sessions in place of face-to-face meetings. Lengthy discussions had been underway for some time considering the potential benefits, risks and ethical issues. These had reached the point where, in the UK, the Family Mediation Council, in September 2016, produced a detailed guidance document for members. The content covers a comprehensive range of advice on ethical, technical and safeguarding matters. On 29 April 2020, the College of Mediators hosted a webinar expert panel discussion about online mediation. It received highly complimentary feedback from college members on its value for them as practitioners. There is little doubt that online video practice was an upcoming contemporary development for practitioners. However, the coronavirus pandemic propelled that evolution to what can be described as 'an idea whose time has come'.

In terms of the coronavirus pandemic, what might the balance be with changes in behaviour, for better or worse, in disputant communications? Similarly, how might practitioners adapt and develop uses of respectfully challenging questions? With regard to the former, we cannot yet know the answers. It seems likely that some disputants in the above categories will continue to follow similar patterns as before. However, given the extraordinary examples of how people have responded generally, with positive and altruistic community caring and volunteering, one can only hope that some of that spirit transfers into dispute behaviours. Perhaps there is a connection here with those ideas expressed by Folger and Bush in their critique of the Western individualist model of mediation:

> The strength of the problem-solving orientation derives from the fact that it stems from and is closely aligned with an individualist ideology that is central to the mainstream culture of the United States. This framework, which applies not only to conflict but to every area of social life, views the human world as made up of radically separate individual beings, of equal worth but with different desires… As an orientation to conflict it embodies the view that conflicts represent problems faced by autonomous individuals in achieving mutual needs satisfaction. (Folger and Bush 1994, pp.12–13)

In raising the possibility of a new non-individualistic ideology, however, they go on to conclude: 'We believe that such an ideology is emerging that views human nature and social interaction in Relational rather than individualist terms, and that gives rise to an orientation to conflict quite different to the problem-solving view' (Folger and Bush 1994, p.15).

Those views based on their work in developing the 'Transformative' mediation model were published over 25 years ago. Could it be that the coronavirus pandemic crisis could revive some of that potential human desire for a more relational society? Here too there are links with the significance of cultural differences and implications for mediation practice. For much more detail on this, see Chapter 3, 'Difference Matters'. Unlike Western individualist cultures, in communitarian/collectivist cultures, the individual can never be more important or powerful than the whole family and faith community. Individual achievement, education, career progress and success are highly valued, but primarily insofar as it reflects well on the family and community. In recent weeks of the lockdown, we have seen a rapid growth of local communities forming volunteer groups and taking care of vulnerable neighbours. It is reminiscent of earlier close-knit pre-industrial village communities, where neighbours all knew each other very well and supported and cared for the vulnerable.

As to the potential influence on practice, it is worth considering that the coronavirus pandemic may stir up greater conflict. For further discussion on recent developments in higher levels of conflict and some potential new ideas for its management, see Chapter 7, 'The Significance of Emotion and High Conflict in Dispute Resolution and the Management of Safe Practice'.

CASE STUDY: Parental behaviour and child welfare priorities

This case example involves a couple where the wife, Sally, moved into a same-sex relationship with the owner of the pre-school playgroup attended by their daughter. The reaction of the father, Tim, was one of rage and included stalking. His reaction was underscored by having been in a relationship for some time with a woman and bonding well with her two children from a former partner. Tragically, the woman died and the maternal grandparents, who had never approved of him, assumed care and control of the children and ended his contact with them. This latest failed relationship was a double loss and grief encounter, and he had homophobic opinions on his wife's new relationship and felt the impact on his own sexual identity.

The first lengthy joint session involved non-stop outpourings of distress, anger, tears and threats from Tim. It was not possible to arrive at even interim arrangements for contact, and he had appointed a solicitor to start court action for a residence order in his favour. At the next session, he arrived early so was seen separately. Asked how things had developed over the last three weeks, he insisted that, apart from having had some weekend staying contact, nothing whatsoever had improved. Seen on her own however, Sally reported a very substantial improvement in Tim's behaviour at handover times. He was far less aggressive and verbally abusive and was willing to consider a regular plan, including more contact days. It seemed almost as if he could not bear to let me know that things had improved in any way, perhaps because to do so would seem to deny his reaction and behaviour at the first meeting. In the joint session, he continued to maintain the view that he wanted a court residence order but would agree on regular contact for the mother. Asked how he would manage day care whilst at work, since he could not afford to give up his job, he said he would engage a nanny or childminder. As a vehicle engineer, his wages would be unlikely to pay for a nanny or even the cost of a childminder. I asked both if, for any unforeseen reason, either parent was physically unable to care for their daughter, temporarily or worse still permanently, who they would most trust to care for her. Sally intervened at this moment to remind Tim that in the past year in their area, a baby in the care of a nanny had died as the result of excessive shaking. That line of needs-led discourse – of discussing the practicalities of childcare alongside full-time work – seemed to be the transitional turning point in negotiations.

They left with an interim agreement that Tim would put the court action on hold temporarily. Sally would agree to him having care most weekday nights and to him dropping the child off to her on his way to and from work. If, as often happened, he was called to an emergency delaying his return, she would feed the child, bathe her and put her in night clothes for him to collect. A follow-up call later confirmed that the arrangements were working well and court action had been withdrawn. This case illustrates how quickly, with help from a mediator, disputants can move from a seriously high conflict and low trust position to a transformative reconnection of child safeguarding principles.

Some more optimistic news

Given the earlier quotes from *The Guardian*, there are now some more positive reports that support the optimism in the above paragraph. The following summaries include examples of comments from an editorial in *The Independent*, just 19 days after the previous *Guardian* editorial:

> Things had been going wrong for Laura and Dave for a good six months before the whole world changed.
>
> 'I honestly thought it was the end,' says Laura. 'The atmosphere was just awful – we'd periodically talk about whether or not we should stay together. There were fights and tears and we'd cling on for a bit longer, but we were miserable. I thought it was only a matter of time.' (Coffey 2020)

The editor comments:

> It may seem strange alongside all the stories of divorce rates soaring once lockdowns are lifted, but Laura and Dave's experience is by no means unique. According to a new survey from charity Relate, 65 per cent of respondents said they currently felt supported by their partner, while 43 per cent of those who live with their partner said the experience of staying at home had brought them closer. ...
>
> Shirlee Kay, a therapist with relationship counselling practice Coupleworks, has noticed some of her clients growing closer during the pandemic. 'Not all the couples I am working with are doing better, but Covid-19 has given couples an opportunity to address issues and see one another differently if they are able

to,' she tells *The Independent*. 'The couples who are doing better are the ones asking themselves what they can learn about here, what is this telling them about what matters in their life.' (Coffey 2020)

This example serves as a useful reminder of how, despite a relationship ending, feelings between couples and related emotional attachments do not usually disappear overnight. Sadly, by the time separation and divorce proceedings have started, especially when characterised by adversarial high conflict, too much emotional and psychological damage has been done for reconciliation to be feasible. In conclusion, in terms of the questions raised at the start of this chapter, it will take some time to begin to know any answers. However, there is no doubt that it will impact on most aspects of life as we have known them, including: world economics; legislation; business; employment; world trade; education; conflict at international, community and family levels; and the NHS. It is acknowledged that case examples provided are centred on family mediation, since that has been my main practice base for more than three decades. Consequently, that gives me a richer source of casework examples to draw on. However, from some involvement with a number of other dispute contexts, I am confident that practitioners will be able to tease out transferable knowledge and implications for other dispute contexts.

In a pre-coronavirus pandemic world, neighbours dispute over noise, parking, children's play; given the enormous upsurge of neighbourhood volunteering and compassionate community care, it is hard to imagine it being just as it was before. In a workplace example, companies will have had to manage the furlough process, bidding for government guaranteed bank loans, even the possibility of winding up the business permanently with consequent income losses to business and workers. It is hard to imagine how life can be quite the same when employers and employees have been forced to collaborate so as to maintain productivity, income and wages. Similar circumstances will probably apply to patient complaints in NHS services. This is not to say that postponed disputes should not rightly be brought back into proper dispute resolution processes. However, it will be interesting to see how attitudes, principles and communication styles on all sides may have changed in the meantime.

If we consider the conclusions listed above, when reflecting on life before and after the coronavirus pandemic, we can but hope that some of the lessons learned, at a national and worldwide level, might just conceivably bring about some dispute resolution changes for the better.

References

Coffey, H. (2020, 26 April) *'Coronavirus Saved My Relationship': Meet the Couples for Whom Lockdown Has Been an Unexpected Blessing.* The Independent. Accessed on 21/09/2020 at https://www.independent.co.uk/life-style/dating/coronavirus-relationship-saved-counselling-break-lockdown-therapy-a9478481.html

Folger, J. and Bush, R. (1994) *The Promise of Mediation. Responding to Conflict Through Empowerment and Recognition.* San Fransisco: Josey-Bass.

Pidd, H. (2020, 7 April) *UK Lawyers Inundated by Divorced Parents Arguing Over Lockdown Custody.* The Guardian. Accessed on 20/09/2020 at https://www.theguardian.com/world/2020/apr/07/lawyers-inundated-by-divorced-parents-arguing-over-lockdown-custody#:~:text=UK%20lawyers%20inundated%20by%20divorced%20parents%20arguing%20over%20lockdown%20custody,-This%20article%20is&text=Lawyers%20have%20been%20inundated%20with,for%20breaking%20existing%20custody%20arrangements

CHAPTER 11

Conclusion

This chapter will highlight some of the key issues covered so far and amplify some interconnected theory and practice issues.

Accountability
Mediation is a publicly accountable professional activity. In the early days of the UK College of Family Mediators, now the College of Mediators, there was significant resistance by some members to the need for supervisory oversight. For me, in such debates, the most effective leveraging was to ask repeatedly: 'To what extent do you consider that mediation is or is not an accountable activity?' Given that it was emerging as a profession and usually charged fees for services, the answer was axiomatically, albeit often begrudgingly, 'yes'. For more detail on the background to this debate and the development of policy and practice see Chapter 2, 'Supervising Mediation Practice', on the supervision of dispute resolution practitioners. As former president Jimmy Carter once said, 'We must adjust to changing times and still hold to unchanging principles'. This quote, for me, usefully sums up the importance of adapting and changing our knowledge and practice as mediation practitioners whilst holding on to the fundamental principles that regulate our practice.

Best practice

Best practice is defined in the Cambridge Dictionary as 'A working method or set of working methods that are officially accepted as being the best to use in a particular business or industry, usually described formally and in detail'.

This definition usefully underscores the exceptional work done over the past two decades by regulatory bodies such as the College of Mediators Professional Standards Committee (PSC) subgroup – sometimes referred to as the 'engine room' of the COM. The pursuit and development of best practice is a professional lifelong journey, not a final destination. The risk with the term best practice is that it could be regarded as a goal to be achieved, an endpoint. In reality, it requires regular periodic review and updating of knowledge and skills in the light of new learning and developments. For example, the regular review of codes of practice undertaken by the PSC is informed by individual practitioners through the constant reflection on their own and others' performance (see Reflective practice below). See also the excellent work of Lang and Taylor and their four-stage developmental pathways, from trainee to novice to experienced practitioner to artistry. They make the point that many practitioners tend to settle at the experienced level and continue to work very competently. One key reason for stopping at this level may well be a consequence of how relatively few mediators earn a full-time living from practice and have to combine it with other activities such as therapy or legal practice. However, in the preface to their book they state wisely that:

> Artistry is not a destination, a place where mediators can settle comfortably, secure in the knowledge that they have attained the highest level of professional competence. Rather, artistry is a journey, a process of exploring and testing the range and application of professional knowledge and skills. (Lang and Taylor 2000, p.xi)

Reflective practice

Readers will be aware of how important I believe reflective practice (RP) to be. The process can operate at two levels in mediation. First, as an external form of auditing such skills as active listening and respectful communication with clients as it is happening. Second, at an internal practice of self-monitoring and development auditing. The first level is covered in detail elsewhere (see Whatling 2012, pp.99–100), so will not be repeated here. The second level involves an internal dialogue, both during and after a session, that audits the effectiveness and quality of skills and strategies together with their associated underpinning knowledge. This 'fly on the wall' self-observation capacity takes time to develop and is difficult for the novice. Nevertheless, the seeds of this capacity can be sown and encouraged by the professional practice consultant. The latter will often encourage the keeping of a 'practice log' by the novice that analyses sessions and is then shared with the PPC. The log is also likely to provide useful additional evidence for the trainee's competence assessment process.

The art of quality RP rests in the ability to engage our 'internal critic' in a positive and constructive dialogue. Such dialogue blames neither clients nor self when things do not go well in a session. Ideally, it is modelled by an experienced PPC, especially after live-observed supervision, as described in Chapter 2. Translated into internal RP, this means first asking, 'What was it that I did that was effective?', and second, asking, 'What else might I have tried and will I try if those circumstances arise again?' Ideally, this should be done by recording the results as an 'aide-mémoire' for follow-up analysis, and developmental goal setting. Being constructively 'easy on the self' should mirror the same constructive process as to how we regard the clients. Practitioners who are inclined to judge some disputants as 'the clients from hell' are engaging in professionally unethical and prejudicial scapegoating. Even at the most experienced practitioner level, there will still be times where we 'lose' the session and/or the clients.

The above model of constructive internal critique, rather than the self or others blame game, inevitably generates valuable insights regarding what could be tried in future in similar cases. At times, we may conclude that in such cases, we as professionals did not yet have the knowledge or skills to be able to manage such highly complex and demanding disputes. As with the above discussion on best practice, it should be regarded as 'work in progress'. In our attempts to work more skilfully with these most difficult and entrenched disputes, we should also be aware that others in the profession are pioneering new models of practice. Their efforts should one day empower our greater capacity to intervene more effectively. Without going into specific detail here, such ongoing work includes dealing with clients with borderline personality disorder, psychologically enmeshed couples, intractable/implacable hostility and parental alienation. The results may, in some instances, require radically different models of practice than most of us have developed thus far. We will have choices. We will either give up trying – not least from a lack of time and income resources – with such cases or keep exploring these new developments. Trainers too should be taking a lead on such initiatives, since being at the 'cutting-edge' of new practice developments is what sells courses and workshops.

Professional self-doubt

Closely linked to reflective practice is the notion of self-doubt (SD). Anecdotal evidence over many years suggests that most people, across a wide range of professions, constantly experience SD about their knowledge and skills. Uncomfortable as that can be, the paradox is that it serves us and our customers well, since it keeps us from complacency and helps us to improve and develop. Interestingly, an online search shows substantially more books and self-help articles on how to beat SD than on its benefits. If a professional experience of self-doubt is at a debilitating level, then it may be appropriate to seek help, either through PPC or perhaps therapy. Unless it is of that level, it may be wiser to seek to 'tame' and manage our SD rather than try to eliminate it. In other words, be careful what you wish for, since you may lose a faithful friend. Most of us will have had the misfortune to meet, and perhaps work with, someone who appeared to live their life without SD. Whilst we may know one or two such people, the probability is that their facade of being self-doubtless is in reality probably in inverse proportion to the size of their SD. There are some useful references to SD online, in particular examples of research on the qualities of therapists. One example explored the relationship between humility and SD, which suggests that they are linked with the qualities of a good therapist:

> 'The whole problem with the world is that fools and fanatics are always so certain of themselves, and wiser people so full of doubts.' This phenomenon – observed in the 1930s by the English philosopher Bertrand Russell – has a technical name, the Dunning-Krüger effect. It refers to the tendency for the worst performers to overestimate their performance, whereas the top performers underestimate their own. The Dunning-Krüger paradox has been found in academic and business settings, but what about in the context of psychotherapy? Is it better to have a confident therapist or one with self-doubt?...
>
> At a time when people tend to think that their value is based on how confident they are and that they must 'sell themselves' in every situation, the finding that therapist humility is an underrated virtue and a paradoxical ingredient of expertise might be a relief. I've certainly found that the findings on the importance of humility resonate with therapists, many of whom have been sceptical of overly confident practitioners in therapy and other fields. Now we need to incorporate the message that humility is an important therapist quality into training and supervision. Part of this will involve a cultural change, so that qualified therapists can act as role-models of humility, to clients and to students, without fear of 'losing face' or authority. (Nissen-Lie 2020)

The focus here is on psychotherapy, but regardless of the fact that a clear distinction has been made between therapy and mediation, it still feels transferable and appropriate to link the two on this issue of SD. Psychotherapist/lecturer/mediator Ilona Mialik illustrated this perfectly when she said 'Where would I be had I not believed I was incompetent?' Having an element of self-doubt can clearly aid in the development of positive qualities such as humility and hard work.

Professional curiosity

The proverb 'curiosity killed the cat' is usually said in order to tell someone that they should not try to find out about something that does not concern them. Professional curiosity, however, provides an ethical standard and framework for mediators that clarifies what should or should not concern them. In particular, it helps stop practitioners from making assumptions and prejudicial judgements; stereotyping; premature outcome problem-solving; or using a categorisation style of listening and labelling from 'inside the box'. Such unprofessional responses occur when busy professionals listen for cues in clients' history and stories. Such cues may trigger 'diagnostic shortcuts' that begin to predict potential stereotypical outcomes and settlements. Experienced practitioners reach a stage of rarely ever hearing a 'new story'. As referred to in previous chapters, it may sound all too familiar to the practitioner, but for the clients, it is usually a unique experience. As such, they are entitled to a bespoke designed model of intervention that is responsive to their particular individual needs. An off-the-peg or one-size-fits-all standard formula is rarely appropriate in mediation. How many times have we heard people say – often in relation with cultural and ethnic difference – 'I'm not prejudiced, I treat everybody the same'? Whilst usually well meant, the reality is that *all people* are uniquely different, and so have a right to be treated differently and individually. Professional curiosity is not idle or nosy curiosity. Its boundaries provide a framework for the construction of professional packaging of interventions, not personal curiosity about odd or unusual personal behaviour disclosures by clients.

Fundamental principles

Sometimes referred to as the 'irreducible principles' of mediation practice, the fundamental principles of mediation practice define ethical codes that guide and determine practitioners' behaviour. They are well described in mainstream dispute resolution literature and provide frameworks for monitoring mediator competence and standards. In particular, they demonstrate respect for client decision-making capacity and autonomy and highlight the difference in respective roles. For example, it is commonly understood that mediators act as the managers of other people's negotiations, whereas clients manage the content agenda and outcome agreements. It is interesting to note that early pioneers in the development of dispute resolution did not invent these principles. They were in reality imported from other long-standing and well-established professions such as counselling and therapy. The task facing early dispute resolution pioneers and writers was to clarify the difference of applying such principles to the outcome objectives of the context. It is perhaps worth highlighting some of these principles that are eminently transferable to mediation. The reason they are explored here is to remind practitioners of the common ground with other helping professions. Trainees from social sciences and therapeutic backgrounds are often reassured that they are not starting again from scratch. For others not from a therapeutic background, they highlight different concepts that can help develop greater background knowledge and inform their practice. Despite the initial disequilibrium experienced by trainees from all backgrounds, I have long held the view that there are few if any differences in the principles, skills and strategies across all social helping contexts. Trainees tend to find that reassuring once they understand the different context of the application.

By way of examples of such transferability, a little-known writer, Felix Biestek, a Jesuit priest, published his work *The Casework Relationship*, often referred to as his 'seven principles', as far back as 1957, summarised as:

> **Individualization** is the recognition and understanding of each client's unique qualities and the differential use of principles and methods in assisting each toward a better adjustment. Individualisation is based upon the right of human beings to be individuals and to be treated not just as a human being but as this human being with his personal differences. (1957, p.25)

This principle speaks to so many of the concepts throughout mediation practice principles as referred to above.

> **Purposeful expression of feelings** is the recognition of the client's need to express his feelings freely, especially his negative feelings. The caseworker listens purposefully, neither discouraging nor condemning the expression of these feelings, sometimes even stimulating and encouraging them when they are therapeutically useful as a part of the casework service. (Biestek 1957, p.35)

Here again is an interesting principle that connects to earlier references to 'managing' as opposed to 'controlling' high emotion. Interestingly, in the early years of developing dispute resolution practice, those two terms were the other way around when describing the role of the mediators. As covered in Chapter 7 on emotion and high conflict, it also challenges the opinions of those practitioners who seek to discourage clients from references to past history and the expression of emotion during meetings.

Acceptance and non-judgementality

Whilst these two are defined separately and in detail by Biestek, they are so well interconnected that they are combined and summarised here as:

> Acceptance is a principle of action wherein the caseworker perceives and deals with the client as he really is, including his strengths and weaknesses, positive and negative feelings, maintaining all the while a sense of the client's innate dignity and personal worth. (Biestek 1957, p.90)
>
> **non-judgementality** – The non-judgemental attitude is a quality of the casework relationship that excludes assigning guilt or innocence or degree of client responsibility for causation of the problems or needs. (Biestek 1957, p.90)

The above two principles are frequently confused and misunderstood. Most commonly, they are taken to imply that we should not make judgements about unacceptable behaviours such as violence, abuse or intimidation. For example, as mediation practitioners, we may be sufficiently concerned about such risks as to make a judgement that mediation should not happen. Nevertheless, the key issue to be understood here is that, despite such professional judgements, an alleged perpetrator's behaviour should not define them as a de facto 'bad person'.

As already stated, mediation is substantially different from therapy. Nevertheless, it has similar characteristics that should be acknowledged. The development of a mutually respectful and trusting professional relationship between the 'help seeker' and 'helper' rests on the quality of interpersonal communications from the earliest point of contact. Congruence between the practitioner's words, tone of voice and non-verbal communication is crucial. Clients are often in a high state of vulnerability and distress or frustration and anger. Their past encounters with other professionals and service providers may not have always been experienced as 'person-centred' or beneficial. Over and above the expectation of professional objectivity, impartiality and trained competence, mediation can be described as an intensively interpersonal activity. Most people know very well when they are being genuinely listened to with understanding and when they are not, whatever the time limits of the encounter. Biestek's principles connect with some long-standing counselling ethics, for example the ideas presented by the highly influential 'non-directive' therapist Carl Rogers' of congruence, unconditional positive regard and empathy.

> If therapy is to occur, it seems necessary that the therapist be, in the relationship, a unified, or integrated, or congruent person. What I mean is that within the relationship he is exactly what he *is* – not a facade, or a role, or a pretence. Unless this congruence is present to a considerable degree it is unlikely that significant learning can occur. (Rogers 1967, p.282)

This reference to 'learning' is intended to describe a mutually beneficial process and helpful outcome for both therapist and client. The former learns more about what is happening to the client and hence is better able to help. The latter learns more about themselves and hopefully, over time, is better able to manage their life.

> Unconditional positive regard. The fourth condition for therapy is that the therapist is experiencing a warm caring for the client – a caring that is not possessive, which demands no personal gratification. It is an atmosphere which simply demonstrates 'I care'; not 'I care for you *if* you behave thus and so.' (Rogers 1967, p.283)

> An empathic understanding. The therapist is experiencing an accurate, empathic understanding of the client's world as seen from the inside. To sense the client's private world as if it were your own, but without ever losing the 'as if' quality – this is empathy, and this seems essential to therapy. (Rogers 1967, p.284)

Empathy is often a misunderstood concept, but the reference to the 'as if' quality is an important reminder of how we should never say 'I know just how you feel'. However similar the client's experience, for example the loss of a close loved one may mirror our own, we can never *know* how it is for them, since they are a unique individual. At best we may be able to begin to imagine how they may be feeling.

To sum up this section, nothing that has been said should be misinterpreted as conflating mediation principles with therapy. It is offered as having some special potential similarities that can inform our work as mediators and hence have some transferable value. As Canadian Prime Minister Justin Trudeau puts it, 'Openness, respect, integrity – these are principles that need to underpin pretty much every other decision that you make'. For me, this quotation usefully sums up the above ideas on similarities and differences between therapy and mediation. Whilst they are significantly different in outcome goals, they have common elements and potential transferability.

Client transitions

Extending the practitioner transitions of Chapter 1, it is worth also considering those of clients, particularly in family mediation contexts. Ending such intimate relationships can be defined as a psycho-social transition and can help with our understanding of the intensity of clients' emotion, pain and distress. This definition conjoins 'psycho', as in the psychological experience, and 'social', referring to the sociological adjustments required. Such major changes may be of similar intensity to former natural transitions, starting with birth and continuing throughout life. For example, detachment from the birth parent, starting and changing schools, starting work, marriage, retirement, bereavement and finally preparing for death. Each stage may require major life changes, frequently together with some inevitable losses and gains. The capacity of a person to manage such loss and grief encounters may well depend on the earliest experience, that of detachment from the birth parent. If, for whatever reason, this stage was unduly traumatic, for example the early loss of the birth parent, it may be that all subsequent life transitions may trigger deeply rooted emotional and psychological symptoms. Particularly severe examples may in some instances account for impasses in moving through the mediation process and in some cases behaviour associated with episodes of mental ill-health. In other words, one or both clients may be apparently unable to stay in the relationship yet be equally unable to leave it – sometimes described as 'psychological enmeshment'. As Mandy Hale said, 'When you are transitioning to a new season of life, the people and situations that no longer fit you will fall away'. This quote illustrates the difference between what might be a difficult yet 'healthy' life transition in comparison with someone whose earliest transitions were for some reason psychologically and emotionally problematic. Hence they tend not to 'fall away'.

Mentoring by informed consent

The definition of mentoring typically relates to work and career contexts. Nevertheless, it includes an interesting reference to psychosocial support, referred to above. This also links well to Chapter 2, 'Supervising Mediation Practice'. However, the aim in Chapter 8, Mediating High Conflict Matters, was to explore its potential for offering it to clients. Controversial as this may seem to some practitioners, the concept stands or falls by the manner in which it is offered. Ethically, this should leave no doubt in the mind of clients that it is their informed choice to accept or decline such help. That level of choice will obviously reflect the nature and quality of the relationship between clients and the practitioner. If the latter works in a directive or evaluative style, informed consent will be compromised. If, however, they have earned respect as someone who empowers clients and believes them as being capable of reconnecting with former abilities to solve their own problems, then it will resonate with facilitative styles of practice.

Finally, I hope that the ideas expressed throughout this book will further dialogue between mediation practitioners across all contexts and at all levels of experience from trainee to artist. Hopefully it will inform, educate, encourage experimentation, challenge and above all stimulate new directions in research and practice for the mutual benefit of dispute resolution and its consumers.

References

Biestek, F. (1957) *The Casework Relationship*. London: Unwin Hyman Inc.

Lang, M. and Taylor, A. (2000) *The Making of a Mediator: Developing Artistry in Practice*. San Francisco: Jossey-Bass.

Nissen-Lie, H. (2020) *Psychiatry and Psychotherapy. Knowledge Virtues and Vices*. Accessed on 28/01/21 at https://aeon.co/ideas/humility-and-self-doubt-are-hallmarks-of-a-good-therapist

Rogers, C. (1967) *On Becoming a Person*. London: Constable & Robinson.

Whatling, T. (2012) *Mediation Skills and Strategies: A Practical Guide*. London: Jessica Kingsley Publishers.

Subject Index

ACAS 122–4
acceptance in mediation 224–7
accountability 217
ADS model 39–40, 41–2, 43–4
alternative dispute resolution (ADR) 18
apologies
    benefits of 112
    case studies 90–2, 108–12
    cultural awareness, and 109–10
    exploration of 94–5
    family mediation, in 90–2
    historical perspective 92–4
    indicators of need 98–102
    litigation, in 112–13
    mediation practice implications 97–102
    mediator strategies for 95–7
best practice 218
BIFF response 184–5
Burch, Noel 33

Carter, Jimmy 217
case studies
    apologies 90–2, 108–12
    coronavirus pandemic 212–14
    cultural awareness 58–9
    family mediation 90–2, 130–1, 134–8, 141–5, 147–8
    gender differences 70–2, 75–7
    high conflict management 160–1
    shuttle mediation 130–1
    transition 19–20
    workplace mediation 75–7

Casework Relationship, The (Biestek) 224
circular questions 166–7
client transactions 227–8
co-mediation
    description of 117
    early developments in 117–19
    gender differences, and 85
    model for 119–22
Code of Practice (College of Mediators) 96–7, 103
Code of Practice (UK College of Family Mediators) 103, 154
College of Mediators (COM) 42, 44, 47, 96–7, 153, 154, 210, 217, 218
Conflict: From Theory to Action (Lulofs and Cahn) 103–4
conjoint mediation and therapy (CoMeT) 148–9
conscious skilled learning stage 34
conscious unskilled learning stage 34
constructive with help from mediation (CWH) behaviours 208
constructive parental separation (CPS) behaviours 206–7
constructs for cultural awareness 61–5
contextually framed questions 167
coronavirus pandemic
    case studies 212–14
    family mediation, and 206–10
    impact of lockdown 204–5
    online sessions during 210–12
    optimism during 214–16

SUBJECT INDEX

cultural awareness
  apologies, and 109–10
  case studies 58–9
  conflict, and 62–5
  constructs for 61–5
  definitions of culture 56–8
  ethnicity, and 66, 67
  high conflict management, and 62–5, 152–3
  individualist and collectivist cultural expectations 62–3
  mediation practice implications 66–7
  problem with generalisations 60–2
  shame and honour issues 65–6
  under-utilisation of mediation 50–60
  useful steps for 67–8
cultural competence 61
cultural fluency 61
cultural intelligence 61
curiosity 222–3

dispute resolution
  family mediation, and 106–8
  reconciliation, and 103–6

Embodied Conflict: The Neural Basis of Conflict and Communication (Hicks) 93–4
emotional management
  forms of emotions 155–6
  high conflict management, and 151–68
  screening for 167–8
  transition to mediation, and 26–31
empathy 226–7

family mediation
  apologies in 90–2
  case studies 90–2, 130–1, 134–8, 141–5, 147–8
  constructive with help from mediation behaviours 208
  constructive parental separation behaviours 206–7
  coronavirus pandemic 206–10
  dispute resolution, and 106–8
  Greek Chorus, and 146–8
  high conflict management in 151–2
  reconciliation, and 102–3, 106–8
  shuttle mediation in 130–1, 132–48
  unconstructive involving legal action behaviours 208–10
  unconstructive parental separation behaviours 207–8
Family Mediation Council (FMC) 96, 210
'Fast Forward: Technologically Enhanced Aggression' (Tannen) 177–8

gender differences
  anecdotal evidence for 77
  approaches to 88
  case studies 70–2, 75–7
  co-mediation, and 85
  controversy over 71–3
  generalisations, and 72–3
  mediation practice implications 82–4
  PPCs in 71, 73, 83
  practice guidance for 84–6
  practitioner knowledge of 86–8
  reasons for exploring 73–5
  scientific basis for 77–82
  workplace mediation, and 75–7
generalisations
  cultural awareness, and 60–2
  gender difference, and 72–3
Getting Together (Fisher and Brown) 200
Greek Chorus 146–8

Haynes, John 18, 40–1, 82–3, 114–15, 210
high conflict management
  BIFF response, and 184–5
  case studies 160–1
  changes in mediation practice 171–2
  client co-operation, and 173–5
  cultural awareness, and 62–5, 152–3
  'do no harm' principle in 165
  family mediation, and 151–2
  informed consent, and 185–6
  life scripts, and 172–3
  media usage 176–8
  mediation practice implications 153–5, 156–60, 161–5
  need for mediation, and 113–14
  neurolinguistics, and 175
  personal narratives in 178–80

high conflict management *cont.*
  pre-mediation assessments 181
  principles in meetings 182–3
  questioning in 165–7
  social media, and 177–8, 183–4
  transition to mediation, and 26–31

informed consent 185–6, 228–9

Jeremy Kyle Show, The 178

learning stages theory 31–6
listening skills 25–6
litigation 112–13

Maslow, Abraham 33
mediation information and assessment meetings (MIAM) 102, 103, 134
mediators own lives
  differences in 191–2
  ideas for managing conflict 192–5
  neglect of 188–91
  recommendations for 195–201
Men Are from Mars, Women Are from Venus (Gray) 77
Myth of Mars and Venus, The (Cameron) 87

National Family Conciliation Council (NFCC) 37–8
National Family Mediation (NFM) 37, 38, 42
neurolinguistics 175
non-judgemental mediation practice 224–7
note taking 24–6

observed practice
  management of 47–51
  Record of Observed Practice form 48–50
  supervising mediation practice, in 45–51
open questions 165–6

personal narratives 178–80
Positions, interests and needs pyramid 192–3

practitioner styles 31–3
pre-mediation assessments 181
principles of mediation 223–4
process options
  co-mediation 85, 117–22
  conjoint mediation and therapy (CoMeT) 148–9
  Greek Chorus 146–8
  shuttle mediation 122–31
  significant others involvement 132–45
  'sitting-with-Nellie' 116–17
professional curiosity 222–3
professional practice consultants/consultation (PPC)
  gender differences, and 71, 73, 83
  supervising mediation practice, and 37, 41–4, 45, 46, 47, 51–5
professional self-doubt 220–2

question usage
  circular questions 166–7
  contextually framed questions 167
  high conflict management, in 165–7
  open questions 165–6
  transition to mediation, and 23–4

reconciliation
  dispute resolution, and 103–6
  family mediation, and 102–3, 106–8
  historical perspective 92–4
Record of Observed Practice form 48–50
reflective practice 219–20

science and gender difference 77–82
self-doubt 220–2
shame and honour issues 65–6
shuttle mediation
  case studies 130–1
  description of 122–4
  family mediation, and 130–1, 132–48
  managing process of 124–30
significant others involvement 132–45
'sitting-with-Nellie' 116–17
social media 177–8, 183–4
standards for supervising mediation practice 38–44

substantive content manager
    (SCM) role 121–2
supervising mediation practice
    development of 37–8
    models of 39–42
    observed practice 45–51
    PPCs in 37, 41–4, 45, 46, 47, 51–5
    standards for 38–44
    training for 38–44
Swindon model 120–1

training
    supervising mediation
        practice, for 38–44
    transition to mediation, for 17–19
transition to mediation
    case studies for 19–20
    difficulties of 19–20
    emotional management 26–31
    high conflict management 26–31
    learning stages theory 31–6
    listening skills 25–6
    note taking 24–6
    practitioner styles 31–3
    psychological experiences of 20–1
    question usage 23–4
    training for 17–19
    transition difficulties 19–20
UK College of Family Mediators
    (UKCFM) 42, 47, 103, 217
unconscious skilled learning stage 34–5
unconscious unskilled learning stage 34
unconstructive involving legal action
    (ULA) behaviours 208–10
unconstructive parental
    separation (UPS) 207–8
underlying process observer
    (UPO) role 121–2

workplace mediation
    case studies 75–7
    gender difference, and 75–7

Author Index

ACAS 123–4
Acland, A.F. 192, 196, 199
Aristotle 180
Augsburger, D.W. 62, 65

Beaulier, M. 29
Benjamin, R. 28
Bert Lance, T. 44
Biestek, F. 224–5
Billig, M. 173
Blue, L. 48
Borisoff, D. 77, 80
Brown, S. 200
Burnham, J. 66, 67
Burns, R. 48
Burrell, I. 176
Bush, R. 211

Cahn, D. 103–4
Cameron, D. 87
Carroll, R. 113
Chin Hu, H. 152–3
Churchland, P.S. 160
Coffey, H. 214, 215
College of Mediators 154

Damasio, A. 160, 161
Dattner, B. 188–9
DJS Research 140

Eddy, B. 179, 184

Fisher, R. 200
Fisher, T. 27–8, 120
Folger, J.P. 62–3, 64, 173, 211

Garfat, T. 39
Gray, J. 77
Greenstein, B. 79

Hale, M. 228
Hargie, O. 25
Harris, T.A. 197
Harris, Q. 66, 67
Haynes, G. 27, 198
Haynes, J. 27, 114, 198, 201
Hicks, T. 93–4, 98, 152, 160

Hoffman, H. 30, 31
Jameson, J.K. 157, 158, 159
Jones, T.S. 62–3, 64, 157, 173

Kadushin, A. 39

Lang, M. 36, 218
LeBaron, M. 56–7, 61, 173
Lulofs, R. 103–4
Luskin, B.J. 82

Maiese, M. 172
Maloney, L. 149
Manchester Evening News 176
Martin, M. 61
Mialik, I. 222

Monk, G. 174, 197

Nelson-Jones, R. 25
Nissen-Lie, H. 221

Pankaj, V. 60
Parkinson, L. 122
Pease, A. 78, 79
Pease, B. 78, 79
Peterson, B. 60, 61, 72
Pidd, H. 204
Pillay, V. 56–7, 61, 173

Randolph, P. 161–2, 164
Richards, C. 29–30
Roberts, M. 29, 117, 122–3, 190
Rogers, C. 226

Schneider, C. 94–5, 97–8, 101
Schön, D. 51–2, 53, 86–7, 171
Schreier, L.S. 158
Smyth, B. 149

Tannen, D. 57–8, 77, 81, 177–8
Taylor, A. 36, 218
Trudeau, J. 227

Ury, W. 200

Vaughn, B.E. 61
Victor, D. 77, 80

Whatling, T. 100, 101, 148, 156, 159, 196, 197, 219
Wilson, A. 112
Winslade, J. 174, 197
Wnuk, A. 98
Wolff, F. 25
Wright, W. 63